Moving into the
Ecumenical Future

Moving into the Ecumenical Future

Foundations of a Paradigm for Christian Ethics

John W. Crossin, OSFS

Foreword by Mitzi J. Budde

PICKWICK *Publications* · Eugene, Oregon

MOVING INTO THE ECUMENICAL FUTURE
Foundations of a Paradigm for Christian Ethics

Pickwick Publications
An Imprint of Wipf and Stock Publishers
199 W. 8th Ave., Suite 3
Eugene, OR 97401

www.wipfandstock.com

PAPERBACK ISBN: 978-1-6667-3753-0
HARDCOVER ISBN: 978-1-6667-9707-7
EBOOK ISBN: 978-1-6667-9708-4

Cataloguing-in-Publication data:

Names: Crossin, John W., author. | Budde, Mitzi, foreword.

Title: Moving into the ecumenical future : foundations of a paradigm for Christian ethics / John W. Crossin ; foreword by Mitzi J. Budde.

Description: Eugene, OR : Pickwick Publications, 2022 | Includes bibliographical references and index(es).

Identifiers: ISBN 978-1-6667-3753-0 (paperback) | ISBN 978-1-6667-9707-7 (hardcover) | ISBN 978-1-6667-9708-4 (ebook)

Subjects: LCSH: Christian ethics. | Ecumenical movement. | Christian union.

Classification: BJ1249 .C76 2022 (print) | BJ1249 .C76 (ebook)

11/09/22

I wish to acknowledge with appreciation the permission from Peeters Press to republish sections from my article "Moving into the Ecumenical Future," *Louvain Studies* 44 (2021) 152–72. These appear in chapter 5.

I also wish to express to the World Council of Churches Publications my gratitude for their permission to publish material from Volume 1 and Volume 3 of the Faith and Order Commission's *Churches and Moral Discernment* series. These are Faith and Order Papers No. 228 and No. 235. They are cited in chapter 9 and chapter 10.

Contents

Foreword

DURING HIS TENURE AS Executive Director of the Washington Theological Consortium from 1998 to 2011, the Rev. Dr. John W. Crossin, OSFS, and I taught ecumenical courses together in a version of Catholic-Lutheran dialogue. After Fr. Crossin left the Washington Theological Consortium to become Executive Director of the Secretariat for Ecumenical and Interreligious Affairs for the U.S. Conference of Catholic Bishops (2011–16), we continued to collaborate. We worked together on the Board of the North American Academy of Ecumenists (NAAE). Father Crossin served as president of the NAAE; I succeeded him a few years later. When I received the Washington Theological Consortium's Figel Ecumenism Award in 2019, Fr. Crossin introduced me before my lecture; when Fr. Crossin received the Figel Ecumenism Award in 2021, I was proudly in attendance for his pandemic virtual award lecture.

Over the years, we have progressed from colleagues to friends to spiritual friends in the Salesian sense (see ch. 2). Father Crossin, my husband (the Rev. John Budde), and I have shared the joys and challenges of our various ministries, discerned the Spirit's stirring of new expressions of vocation, and prayed through various personal crises. We've celebrated each other's successes and critiqued one another's drafts; indeed, we discussed the early seeds of this book around the dinner table. Feasting, storytelling, and laughing together reflect our spiritual friendship as well.

Father Crossin accurately describes himself as an "optimistic ecumenist." He is the most ecumenically committed person I've ever met. In his various ministries, he has contributed to many of the national and international ecumenical accomplishments of our time. Pope Francis appointed Fr. Crossin as a Consultor to the Pontifical Council for Promoting Christian Unity for a six-year term in 2014. He was a key contributor to the Lutheran-Catholic document, *Declaration on the Way*, and served as a member of the Pontifical Council's team for the Joint Working Group with the World Council of Churches. He has authored four prior theological books.

This book, *Moving into the Ecumenical Future*, is the pinnacle of Fr. Crossin's multi-faceted ecumenical vocation. Here, Fr. Crossin situates ecumenical ethics at the crossroads of ministry, scripture, and spirituality. This is not the traditional philosophically-based approach, but rather, this is an integrated, multi-dimension approach that is pastoral, biblical, theological, scientific, and relational, in continuity with the tradition and grounded in prayer and the sacraments. Father Crossin's specialty in VE is informed by his Salesian Spirit-centered spirituality and his extensive pastoral experience in various Roman Catholic parishes and at the Saint Luke Institute in Silver Spring, Maryland. The book uses ecumenical dialogue achievements to propose a paradigm for a convergence on ethics.

In his characteristic self-effacing and humble style, Fr. Crossin cites an impressive array of scholarly voices to elucidate his line of reasoning in each chapter. This broadened my knowledge of the literature, yet my favorite parts are the "reflection" sections where Fr. Crossin demonstrates how those scholars advance his unique perspective—see, for example, "Embodying Virtues" in chapter 8 and "Crossin's Moral Paradigm Proposal" in chapter 9.

This book matters for professional ecumenists because it offers a new step forward on moral discernment. Drawing upon the international ecumenical agreement, *The Joint Declaration on the Doctrine of Justification*, this is a visionary and exploratory proposal to draw upon the differentiated consensus already achieved to construct a common moral paradigm "that will guide Christian communities as they work together to resolve new ethical issues or revisit old ones" (ch. 10). This constructive theology has the potential to reinvigorate the charism for ecumenism in the church today.

If you are a Christian seeking to live your faith ethically in the twenty-first century in continuity with Scripture and the faith of the church, this book is for you as well. In it, you will encounter the voice of a wise teacher, an experienced pastor, a brilliant academician, an ecumenical enthusiast, and a discerning spiritual leader.

Father Crossin gently challenges all Christians to listen for the Spirit's guidance and "get out of ourselves and our worlds and encounter other Christians, learn from them, and become holy" (ch. 10). His invitation is to the church catholic; he addresses Roman Catholics, Lutherans, Methodists, Anglicans, Reformed, Orthodox, Baptists, and others.

Moving into the Ecumenical Future calls us all to grow together in our practice of the faith and our discernment around moral matters, centered on Christ and the virtue of love. This book envisions a future-oriented relational journey into a more unified Christian witness to the world, grounded in Scripture and the mystery of the holy Trinity.

Mitzi J. Budde,
Virginia Theological Seminary
January 21, 2022

Acknowledgments

I WISH TO THANK V. Rev. Lewis Fiorelli, OSFS, Provincial Superior, for his ongoing encouragement of this book project with its roots in the Salesian Spirituality of our Congregation. Likewise, I wish to thank my Oblate confreres for their ongoing encouragement especially Joseph Chorpenning, OSFS, William Metzger, OSFS, Mark Mealey, OSFS, and all those Oblates who resided at Brisson Hall in Washington, DC, the last few years. I owe a debt of gratitude to the Carmelites at Whitefriars Hall for their hospitality while I was researching and writing the text. In particular, I would mention Quinn Conners, O. Carm., Nepi Willemsen, O. Carm., Dan O'Neill, O. Carm., and the "student brothers." As Dr. Budde mentions in her *Foreword*, many of the ideas in the book originated in table discussions with those just mentioned.

I also want to acknowledge the "Ethics Professors" Faculty Group, and the "Science and Religion Group," of the Washington Theological Consortium. The deep roots of some of the integration that I attempt in this book go back to the meetings of these groups while I was Director of the Consortium.

Particular thanks go to Sheila Garcia and Dr. Mitzi Budde for their feedback as I was writing. Their suggestions helped me to clarify my thinking along the way and to correct mistakes I made whether intellectual or grammatical. I also wish to express my gratitude to Pastor John Budde for our discussions over the years of particular and often difficult pastoral questions.

I am grateful to my editor at Wipf and Stock, Dr. Charlie Collier, and his colleagues who responded so quickly to my inquiries and encouraged this work.

Finally, I want to acknowledge the support of my brothers and sister and their families as I developed and then acted on my ideas. They were very patient in listening to the explanations of what I was trying to do. I also want to mention my parents whose influence, after all these years, is still quite evident in my life.

Abbreviations

ARCIC   Anglian-Roman Catholic International Commission

DEM   *Dictionary of the Ecumenical Movement.* Edited by Nicholas Lossky et al. Geneva: WCC, 2002.

DSE   *Dictionary of Scripture and Ethics.* Edited by Joel B. Green. Grand Rapids: Baker Academic, 2011.

DOTW   *Declaration on the Way: Church Ministry and Eucharist.* Committee on Ecumenical and Interreligious Affairs, United States Conference of Catholic Bishops, and Evangelical Lutheran Church in America. Minneapolis: Augsburg Fortress, 2015.

F&O   Faith and Order Commission

JDDJ   *Joint Declaration on the Doctrine of Justification.* The Lutheran World Federation and the Roman Catholic Church. Grand Rapids: Eerdmans, 2000.

NCBC   *The New Collegeville Bible Commentary.* Edited by Daniel Durken. Collegeville, MN: Liturgical, 2017.

NDT   *New Dictionary of Theology.* Edited by Joseph A. Komonchak et al. Wilmington, DE: Glazier, 1987.

PBC   *The Paulist Biblical Commentary.* Edited by Jose Enrique Aguilar Chiu et al. New York: Paulist, 2018.

PCPCU   Pontifical Council for Promoting Christian Unity

VE   Virtue Ethics

WCC   World Council of Churches

WDCE   *The Westminster Dictionary of Christian Ethics*. Edited by James F. Childress and John Macquarrie. Philadelphia: Westminster, 1986.

WTW   "Walking Together on the Way: Learning to Be the Church— Local, Regional, Universal." Agreed Statement of ARCIC III.

Introduction

IN OVER FORTY YEARS of ministry, including twenty years working directly for Christian unity, I have learned that ecumenism and ministry are about our relationships with God and relationships with people. Central to these relationships, and what I emphasize in this volume, are the guidance of the Holy Spirit, the commitment to follow Jesus, the importance of spiritual growth, and the necessity of ethical dialogues with mutual respect.

The book is a direct outcome of my work on the *Declaration on the Way: Church, Ministry, and Eucharist*. This declaration is a compilation of agreements and remaining differences on church, ministry, and Eucharist from Lutheran-Catholic dialogues throughout the world. The final section indicates several ways that Lutherans and Catholics might "express and advance the growing communion" between them. One section reads:

> Lutherans and Catholics will continue to advance on the path toward unity by addressing the moral issues that are often thought to be church dividing in the same spirit of mutual respect and commitment to unity characterized by their work on issues of justification, church ministry, and eucharist.[1]

During a retreat for prayer and discernment at Holy Cross Trappist Abbey I realized that I might have a contribution to make to such a mutually respectful and committed discussion. This book is one result of this discernment.

1. *DOTW*, 122.

The book is directed especially to those engaged in formal and informal ecumenical dialogues whether on the local, regional, national, or international levels and to colleagues who participate in theological and ethical societies. I believe that discussions of ecumenical ethics should go beyond Lutherans and Catholics to include Methodist, Reformed, and Anglican colleagues from those communions that have endorsed the *Joint Declaration on the Doctrine of Justification*. Orthodox, Baptist, and other colleagues have contributions to make as well.[2] I have cited works from members of these communities throughout this book. Moral theology/Christian ethics is of practical interest to all Christians. I hope this text is accessible and helpful and can be read with benefit by Christians with a bit of theological background who are seeking to grow in faithfulness to Christ and love for one another.[3]

Ecumenical ethics stands at the crossroads of several disciplines including spirituality, biblical studies, ecclesiology, neurobiology, developmental psychology, and pastoral theology. Ecumenical ethics is complex. It is difficult/impossible for any one person to grasp thoroughly all these disciplines. I recommend substantive and critical dialogue among experts from the various disciplines. The decision-makers noted in the essays in volume 1 of *Learning from Traditions* of the Faith and Order Commission of the World Council of Churches will depend on these in-depth discussions by experts for their discernments.[4] When I touch on topics that are beyond my areas of expertise, I will tend to quote and reference such experts more extensively.[5]

In this volume we will be trying to do four things:

First, we will identify some necessary "elements" for any paradigm for ecumenical ethics. These elements—elaborated in the chapters cited—include:

2. See Harmon, *Baptists, Catholics, and the Whole Church*; Special Commission, *For the Life of the World*. *For the Life of the World* is discussed by six authors in the September 2020 issue of *Ecumenical Trends*. Ecumenical Patriarch Bartholomew mentions that "different ways in which churches respond to moral problems are not necessarily insurmountable, since churches witness to the gospel in different context" in his recent remarks at the National Council of Churches.

3. Those unfamiliar with or needing a review of the basics of ecumenism might consult the ecumenical sections of the websites of their traditions. They might begin with Crossin, "Moving Forward in the Spirit," 60–64.

4. See chapter 9 below.

5. The use of "we" connotes that this book is usually an interaction of author and reader. I say I when stating my views. My own additions to quotes and other items in the text will appear in brackets.

1. A focus on ongoing conversion to Christ and the guidance of the Holy Spirit and the realization that we will never comprehend the mystery of the Trinity and can always grow in our understanding and practice of our Christian faith (chapter 1);

2. Concern for pastoral experience with a focus on the uniqueness of everyone made in God's image (chapters 2 and 8);

3. Emphasis on spiritual growth and especially on discernment of God's will (chapters 2 and 9);

4. A conviction that a Christian ethic should rely on prayerful contemplation as much as rational arguments (chapters 2, 4, and 10);

5. Reverence for and inclusion of our Jewish heritage especially the Old Testament and the realization that we interpret our Jewish heritage through the teaching of Jesus and the New Testament; (chapter 3)

6. The importance of relationships and the contributions of relational theologies; (chapter 4)

7. The conclusions of formal ecumenical dialogues (chapter 5);

8. Recognition that spiritual/moral growth goes through stages which include an emphasis on justice and law that is sublated into subsequent stages that emphasize virtues especially loving (chapter 7);

9. A prayerful understanding of Jesus's teaching especially on the Love of God and Neighbor, the Sermon on the Mount, the Commandments, and the Works of Mercy (Matt 25: 31–46) (chapter 10);

10. A spiritual focus on the central sacraments of baptism and Eucharist and as much focus on the eternal banquet as on the Last Supper (chapter 10).

The chapters of this book are meant to provide deeper insight into these elements and encourage further consideration of them in formal dialogues as foundational for ecumenical ethics.

Second, we will emphasize spiritual ecumenism and the importance of the guidance of the Holy Spirit and the teaching and example of Jesus in developing paradigm(s) for ecumenical ethics. We will rely particularly on the Salesian spirituality of Francis de Sales (1567–1622) and Jane de Chantal (1572–1641) with its emphasis on gentleness and respect for the individual. Francis de Sales was criticized by more militant Catholics of his era because of his respect for his Calvinist opponents.

Third, we suggest that Virtue Ethics is one important paradigm that includes these elements. VE offers a biblically based, philosophically, theologically, spiritually, and pastorally coherent moral paradigm that supports Christian unity and that encourages the baptized to follow the Gospel daily. VE already has exponents in Catholicism, Orthodoxy, and the Protestant traditions.[6] As with any major theological school, VE has many variations/ approaches around a common core.

Fourth, we explore how receptive ecumenism, the differentiated consensus exemplified in the JDDJ, and discernment might be used to move toward moral consensus.[7] Christian communities are already becoming more sensitive to the work of the Holy Spirit in other Christian communities and the need to adopt other traditions' best practices. Likewise, the 2017 Statement of the Finnish Lutheran-Catholic Dialogue presents a differentiated consensus on church, Eucharist, and ministry. Such efforts point the way to some consensus on moral principles and moral issues. Here we begin work to identify *core elements* of any moral paradigm and the scope of differences amidst unity. This work is the beginning of a process of developing (a) moral paradigm(s) that can be continued by groups working together perhaps even by an international working group.

Overview of the Chapters

Each chapter develops foundational elements for an ecumenical paradigm.

Chapter 1 discusses the role of the Holy Spirit in the context of recent discussions of the Trinity, of the rise of the Pentecostal/Charismatic movements, and of Salesian spirituality. The Spirit has been guiding the ecumenical movement since its beginning in 1910. The fruits of this guidance can be seen vividly in the Second Vatican Council with its Decree on Ecumenism and in the results of the current ecumenical dialogues.

Chapter 2 discusses pastoral ministry and discernment. It is appropriate to build our approach to an ecumenical ethics at the crossroads of ministry, scripture, science, and spirituality. This approach recognizes what

---

6. See Crossin, "Virtue as an Ecumenical Ethic," 28–31; Crossin, *What Are They Saying about Virtue?*

7. See Witherup, *Galatians*, 51–60, for a pastorally oriented summary of justification and the *JDDJ*. It should be noted that the model of differentiated consensus has had a wider impact as, for example, in "The Word of God in the Life of Church," the final report of the dialogue between the Catholic Church and the Baptist World Alliance (2006–10).

is already happening in the ecumenical movement: common prayer for the Spirit's guidance, working together to build unity at home and in society, attention to modern sciences, and a growing interest in spirituality and spiritual growth.

This discussion flows into chapter 3 which focuses on the Bible and biblical ethics. The main foundation for moral reflection, pastoral work and spiritual care is the Scriptures, especially the New Testament. The great commandment of love (e.g., Matt 22), the Sermon on the Mount/Plain, the teaching of Matthew 25, and the Ten Commandments are cornerstones of Christian activity in the world. Christians—praying as Jesus did—often seek divine guidance in living out his teachings. The Bible is central to Christian prayer, moral formation, and Christian action.

Christian biblical scholars argue that it is important to consider the work of Jewish biblical scholars in any exposition of the Scriptures. Collaboration between Scripture scholars and Christian ethicists needs to continue to go deeper.

Chapter 4 discusses relationality first in the personal relationships that are so crucial to ecumenism and then from the point of view of systematic theology and philosophy. We live in a relational universe. In this age of Einstein's theory of relativity, of "string theory," and of "spacetime," we see that the whole universe speaks of relationships. Scientific findings considered critically are part of the context in which we develop our philosophies and theologies of relationality.

Chapter 5 looks at recent ecumenical dialogues. The ecumenical movement has made great progress during the century of its existence. A prime example is the *JDDJ*. This document with its approach referred to as "differentiated consensus" has been widely approved. This chapter points primarily to recent agreements and ongoing dialogues which set the stage for considering moral paradigms.

Chapter 6 considers paradigms. What a paradigm is in general, the need for paradigms, how paradigms change, and the shifting paradigms in ecumenism are some of the topics presented. Since the earliest times, Christians have sought to be consistent in their moral teaching. Jesus did not teach on every topic of moral consequence and new moral questions have presented themselves over the centuries. Christians have borrowed critically from the dominant philosophies of their time in seeking consistency. Christian ethicists, however, focus on Christ and the virtue of love as central to a common ethical paradigm.

Chapter 7 has a detailed discussion of the important paradigm of VE. The emphasis on virtue and growth in virtue is a positive one in contrast to an exclusive emphasis on right/wrong. Growth in virtue involves becoming a certain kind of person. This chapter continues the discussion of the virtue of love begun in chapter 6. Love itself can develop over time as we see in the *stages of loving* found in Francis de Sales' *Treatise on the Love of God*. In this context, the chapter moves on to discuss some findings of developmental psychology and also the importance of law. The process of moral development allows for the presence of moral rules/moral absolutes within the paradigm of VE. This leads to a discussion of the relationship of law to a Christian virtue paradigm.

Chapter 8 considers the impact of neurobiology on our moral thinking and then considers a standard analysis of moral actions. The chapter then moves from the inner peace Jesus offers to peacebuilding to consideration of the importance of honesty and love for all, even enemies. The setting for moral actions is the moral community which is seeking to follow Christ.

In chapter 9, we review three—all appeared in 2021—documents on Moral Discernment from the Faith and Order Commission of the World Council of Churches. We also examine Michael Root's new overview of ecumenical morality, the book edited by Hak Joon Lee and Tim Dearborn containing essays on sixteen moral issues, and John W. O'Malley's essay on the development of doctrine in Catholicism. At the conclusion of the chapter, *I propose that some of the signatories of JDDJ sponsor a Working Group that will seek to construct a common moral paradigm.*[8]

Chapter 10 offers a discussion of "Foundations of an Ecumenical Paradigm for Moral Teaching." The chapter: repeats my call for a Working Group to develop an ecumenical paradigm; reviews some implications in speaking of a "Paradigm;" notes that our journey toward the heavenly banquet is grounded in the central sacraments of baptism and Eucharist; refers to the ten elements for an ecumenical paradigm for Christian ethics mentioned in this introduction; advocates for four central scriptural elements in any ecumenical moral paradigm; discusses the important Faith and Order document *Churches and Moral Discernment 4: Facilitating Dialogue to Build Koinonia* and in particular "Part 4, A Tool to Understand Moral Disagreement and Facilitate Dialogue to Build Koinonia"; and delineates

---

8. The signatories are the Roman Catholic Church, the Lutheran World Federation, the World Methodist Council, the Communion of Reformed Churches, and the Anglican Communion.

general categories into which moral issues might fall with the help of differentiated consensus, Pope Francis' "Polarities" in the church, and my reflections on human "Universalizing" tendencies.

Personal Reflections

I am sure that my upbringing in middle class Philadelphia and my education in mathematics, psychology and theology have influenced the reflections presented in this volume. Likewise, the fact is that in the 1950s I played sports in the neighborhood almost every day but never thought to invite my Protestant neighbors to the Catholic Church—nor did they invite me to theirs.

Things began to change when the Second Vatican Council opened. Our family had moved, and we were in a parish that adopted the Council changes in the liturgy readily and had a priest on staff who explained what changed and why. I have lived my adult life in the religious community of the Oblates of Saint Francis de Sales and have been deeply affected by these changes and subsequent events up to the present moment.

Official Catholic participation in the ecumenical movement was a result of the Council. I hope that the reflections in this volume point toward moral consensus. A century of dialogue and collaboration has brought the Christian churches closer together.

In two recent articles, I contend that ecumenically-minded Christian churches are now moving toward full communion.[9] Part of this movement is consideration of the differences among Christian traditions on some ethical issues. We see this movement for example in the International Anglican-Roman Catholic dialogue and in the publications on Discernment of the Faith and Order Commission of the World Council of Churches. I believe that the Christian traditions should seek to develop a common moral paradigm(s).

The four chapters that follow this Introduction will discuss the spiritual, pastoral, biblical and relational roots of a common paradigm.

---

9. See Crossin, "Moving into the Ecumenical Future," 152–72; Crossin, "Will Christian Unity Come?," 18–23.

1

The Holy Spirit

THE HOLY SPIRIT HAS been guiding the ecumenical movement since the beginning. As we discuss ecumenical ethics, we will need this guidance more than ever.

The Spirit has been guiding these efforts since at least 1910. An invitation from an Anglican friend to Catholic archbishop Bonomelli of Cremona, Italy, to attend the 1910 International Missionary Congress in Edinburgh, Scotland, could not be accepted in those days of continuing interchurch conflicts. The archbishop sent positive greetings. At the beginning of the Congress, these were read publicly by his friend to the assembled Protestant and Anglican delegates. They were well received.

Significantly, the archbishop shared with a group of young priests his perception that they should follow the ecumenical movement because it was important. One of those priests, Angelo Roncalli, upon election as Pope John XXIII in late 1958, announced the Second Vatican Council (1962–65) in January 1959 at the close of a prayer service for Christian unity. One of the main topics of the Council was to be Christian unity.[1] The Council was a major event that led to renewed interest in the work of the Holy Spirit in an Ecumenical Council and in the church.

The Spirit seems to have been at work over several decades in the ecumenical movement and in moving the Catholic Church in an ecumenical direction. The 1999 *Joint Declaration on the Doctrine of Justification*

---

1. Delaney, "Cremona," 418–31.

between the Lutheran World Federation and the Catholic Church is an important result of this divine guidance.[2]

This chapter considers contexts for the work of the Spirit. It begins by considering personal experiences of the Spirit, continues by noting the emphasis on experience in the growing Pentecostal Movement worldwide, follows this with a summary of the renaissance of theological reflection on the Trinity, and finishes with some ecumenical reflections.

Personal Experience of the Spirit

We begin this section on the Holy Spirit by asking: How do we experience the Holy Spirit working in our lives? Upon consulting several friends and my own experience, we noted five ways in particular:

> As wisdom—the Spirit guides us, sometimes in quite surprising ways, to say or do the appropriate thing.
>
> As empowerment—when we are aware of our weaknesses and limitations the Spirit gifts us with strength and courage to do what needs to be done.
>
> As openness—to people, to ideas, to new ways of seeing reality and seeing beyond reality. The ecumenical movement calls for openness and for the courage to move beyond our fears to hear and respond to others.
>
> As freedom—not freedom as the multiplication of choices but the freedom to do God's will. This includes "choosing well" and following through. We know that unity is Christ's will for the church. Our follow-through is needed.
>
> As healing—the grace of the Spirit can heal life's deepest hurts and bring peace to ourselves and our world.[3]

Having looked at our own experiences of the Spirit, we would be remiss if we did not give some consideration to the fast-growing and diverse Pentecostal Movement that is prominent in many parts of the world.

---

2. See *JDDJ*.
3. Crossin, *Walking in Virtue*, 3–4.

Pentecostal and Charismatic Christians

Personal experiences of the Holy Spirit working in our lives, while common to many Christians, are characteristic of Pentecostal and Charismatic Christians. These Christians are noted for sharing their experience of the Spirit with others.

Pentecostals are often referred to as Traditional Pentecostals—those having roots in early twentieth century American Christianity—and New Pentecostals of more recent origin often found in the Global South. Charismatic Christians are members of church traditions such as Methodist, Catholic, Episcopalian, Lutheran, and Reformed who have had an experience of the Holy Spirit.

Key elements for all these Christians are: a reliance on the Scriptures, an experience of baptism in the Holy Spirit, the consciousness of personal "gifts of the Spirit," an openness to spiritual healing of soul and sometimes of body, deeper prayer, an emphasis on community praying together, and witnessing to others about their Christian faith. There is a strong affective element in Pentecostal/Charismatic prayer and often great enthusiasm for sharing "what the Spirit has done for me."[4]

Classical Pentecostals in the United States have moved toward becoming Pentecostal churches with some church structures. Charismatic Christians from varied Christian traditions already have the ecclesiology of their churches.[5] And "New Pentecostals" often are in individual church communities. Many Pentecostals think of themselves more as a Movement than as a church. While there are a good number of important Pentecostal theologians, Pentecostals overall tend to value personal experience and sharing of one's faith over theological reflection.[6]

Particularly helpful to the pastoral/spiritual reflections in this volume is the excellent Report of the Sixth Phase of the International Catholic-Pentecostal Dialogue (2011–15) entitled "Do Not Quench the Spirit: Charisms in the Life and Mission of the Church."[7] This is an important document on

4. See Vondey, "The Unity"; Vondey, *Pentecostal Theology;* Rausch, "Ecumenism for a Global Church," 199–202; Koch, "Pentecostals."

5. The new Catholic Charismatic Renewal International Service [CHARIS] is part of the Dicastery for Laity, Family, and Life at the Vatican.

6. I would note the theological and pastoral reflections of the members of the American Society for Pentecostal Studies in their journal *Pneuma* and their annual meetings provide significant insight into the movement.

7. See the bibliography for a link to this document.

a somewhat neglected topic, one important for Christian unity. A few key elements are:

> Freely and sovereignly bestowed by the Holy Spirit, charisms equip believers to participate in God's saving plan and to praise and glorify God. (no. 9)[8]

> Both the more extraordinary charisms (such as healings, miracles, prophecy, and tongues) and those that seem more ordinary (such as service, teaching, exhortation, contribution, administration, and acts of mercy) are vital for the life and mission of the Church. (no. 11)

> Charisms are gifts of the risen and ascended Lord Jesus through the Holy Spirit (cf. Eph 4:8–12). Christ's presence in the world is revealed not only in his works of power but also in the weakness, poverty, and suffering that is part of the human condition (2 Cor 12:9). Even the most powerful charisms do not exempt Christians from taking up the cross and embracing the cost of discipleship. (no. 13)

An Anglican theologian friend, who is also a charismatic Christian, remarked to me several times that significant elements of the Pentecostal Movement were gradually moving in an ecumenical direction. He believed that a sharing of charisms would be mutually beneficial. This is my belief as well.[9]

The dialogue text goes on to discuss in some detail the charisms of prophecy, healing, and discernment. A significant point mentioned but sometimes not stressed sufficiently is that those with charisms are responsible to the community and should be responsive to those who exercise pastoral leadership (nos. 91–104).

"*The exercise of charisms, when accompanied by holiness of life, glorifies God and empowers the spread of the gospel to the ends of the earth (cf. Acts 1:8)*" (no. 106). This volume contends that the variety of charisms given to Christians in all traditions will be necessary in developing ecumenical ethics.

---

8. Page numbers or paragraph numbers are provided for the convenience of the reader.

9. See the ecumenically oriented programming of the Catholic Charismatic Renewal found at www.adc.cmax.tv.

Pastoral Call

Given the importance of charisms, we might consider a little further God's call to pastoral ministry. Edward P. Hahnenberg offers Catholics and Christian colleagues a helpful reflection on discerning the call from the Spirit to ministry and the sharing of one's gifts—whether full or part-time.

His first chapter is on the "Call."

> Discernment, then, is not a spiritual treasure hunt. It is less about looking out and more about listening within. To discover a calling is to hear a certain harmony between *who* I am as a child of God, on one hand, and how I live and what I do, on the other. When faith-filled people say that they have discovered their vocation, they are not saying that they have found some hidden plan. Rather, they are saying that they have felt a profound resonance between their deepest sense of themselves before God and a particular path forward.[10]

His subsequent chapter on the Holy Spirit is most enlightening especially regarding the charisms or gifts of the Spirit mentioned above. Part of coming into ministry is to discern carefully what gifts God has given to us for ministry and what gifts we do not have. Often it is our spiritual friends who can see some of our gifts better than we see them ourselves. On the other hand, author Parker Palmer contends that "burnout is not about giving too much, it's about giving too little. It's about trying to give what we do not have."[11]

Hahnenberg's emphasis in his final chapter on the trinitarian nature of ministry can help overcome a divide in understanding and emphasis between calls to ordained or non-ordained ministry. Differences in self-understanding can be evident in church circles between clergy and laity. The bigger picture that subsumes differences in emphasis or concern is: "Like the three persons of the Trinity, ministers find their identity and purpose in relationship." Furthermore, "we can say that evangelization today is as much about connecting with others as it is about communicating. It is as much about *presence* as *proclamation*."[12]

The 2017 Report of the Lutheran Catholic Dialogue Commission for Finland also points to the trinitarian context of ecumenical ministry. This

---

10. Hahnenberg, *Theology for Ministry*, 14.

11. Hahnenberg, *Theology for Ministry*, 84.

12. Hahnenberg, *Theology for Ministry*, 117, 124.

statement quotes Cardinal Walter Kasper's *Harvesting the Fruits* which reads in part:

> The dialogues of the Roman Catholic Church with Lutherans, Reformed, Anglicans and Methodists ". . . are united in agreement that the Church as people of God, Body of Christ and Temple of the Holy Spirit, is in intimate relation to the economy of the Trinity. All four dialogues confirm the unique mediation of Jesus Christ and the role of the Holy Spirit as primary agent within the Church. In particular, the vision of the Church as communion—in keeping with the pattern in the Holy . . . Trinity—has become increasingly central in all dialogues. Focusing on the notion of the Church as koinonia/communion not only highlights the richness of the nature of the Church, but also helps in dealing with significant issues of historical conflict."[13]

Before we move on to further thoughts on the work of the Holy Spirit, it is good to consider some recent reflections on the Trinity. What follows will provide a context for our reflections on the guidance of the Holy Spirit. But it will only skim the surface of the burgeoning literature on the Trinity.[14]

The Holy Trinity

The internationally known Australian scholar Gerald O'Collins offers a concise and readable summary of the theology of the Trinity in the revised second edition of his book *The Tripersonal God: Understanding and Interpreting the Trinity*. He says:

> In reflecting on their trinitarian faith, Christian believers have the task of looking at and drawing on (1) the historical experience of salvation which the scriptures record and which teachers in the church have interpreted through the centuries; (2) the testimony of public worship; and (3) the experience of practicing discipleship today.[15]

Trinitarian faith expresses itself in knowledge, worship, and action.[16]

13. Lutheran Catholic Dialogue Commission for Finland, *Communion in Growth*, no. 2.

14. See chapter 5 on the *JDDJ* and receptive ecumenism for reference to an underlying trinitarian emphasis in their approaches to moving toward Christian unity.

15. O'Collins, *The Tripersonal God*, 1–2.

16. O'Collins, *The Tripersonal God*, 3.

O'Collins' Chapter Ten is on *Trinitarian Persons and Action*. Its emphasis is on relationality in the Trinity. "What I am saying here about the relational aspect of being a person and of personhood being *interpersonhood* commands, I believe, a fairly wide degree of acceptance. In the case of the Trinity, the relational aspect is both unique and crucial" lest one fall into "multiple gods."[17] In this context, O'Collins discusses the *koinonia* or perfect communion and *perichoresis* or mutual indwelling of the persons of the Trinity.

This emphasis on relationality in the Trinity—perfect communion and mutual indwelling—points toward the relationality which will be a foundational element for ecumenical ethics. Hahnenberg mentions above that relationships are key to pastoral ministry as well.

O'Collins discusses *The Personal Existence of the Holy Spirit* (chapter 9) quite thoroughly. Interestingly, he mentions that he will distinguish between:

> God's actions (which are common to all three divine persons) and those actions' visible terms, which allow us to distinguish between the three persons. Apropos of the Spirit's action in the world beyond the Christian community, one must also (or even primarily) think of the term as eschatological. It will take the end of all things and all history to let us discern the visible term of the Spirit's full activity on the world and the cosmic scene.[18]

Our ecumenical ethics must realize and include the work of the Spirit in all the Christian communities and even beyond these communities. At the end of time, we will see the fullness of the Spirit's work. Now we can detect some parts of this work and include them in our ecumenical ethics.

Our ecumenical work should be balanced between focus on the past and on the future. The question of this orientation to the future will recur on pp. 26–27.

The Evangelical-Catholic collection, *Knowing the Triune God*, presents a series of diverse essays which add an important emphasis to our reflections:

> What is it, then, that unifies the three parts [of the book]? It is, we think, the book's central theme: knowing the triune God is inseparable from participating in a community and its practices—a participation which Christians link with the work of God's Holy Spirit. . . .

17. O'Collins, *The Tripersonal God*, 177.
18. O'Collins, *The Tripersonal God*, 169.

> But what Christians say about the triune God cannot be adequately explicated without reference to what Christians most characteristically do in worship and obedience to that God.[19]

The editors contend that lines between denominations and even lines in the closely guarded academic world are now being crossed in this renewal of focus on the Trinity.[20] This renewed focus is evident in ecumenical documents such as the *JDDJ* where paragraph 15, the key statement of consensus, begins with reference to the persons of the Trinity.[21]

The Cambridge Companion to the Trinity offers twenty-three essays on trinitarian topics by distinguished experts from different Christian traditions. These essays are mostly focused on the Reformation and on contemporary theologians' work on the Trinity. They expand further our comprehension of the renewed emphasis on the Trinity.

> Recently, a spate of books and articles on the Trinity by Catholic, Orthodox and Protestant theologians have restored this neglected Christian doctrine to its rightful place. These works have not only retrieved classical teachings on the Trinity through serious historical research but have also given the lie to the claim that the trinitarian dogma is nothing more than abstruse metaphysics and a conundrum of "higher mathematics" of one-equals-three and vice versa. They have shown how trinitarian theology is necessary for a full understanding of such burning issues as the nature of the human person, suffering, sexism, ecology, social and economic justice, interreligious dialogue, and so on.[22]

Editor Peter C. Phan goes on to say that the development of this doctrine has not been linear despite organic metaphors that imply steady growth. There has been "growth, decline, eclipse, retrieval" and so forth. Phan reviews key elements in this development. One of the final points that he makes is that "It took a [Karl] Barth [Reformed] and a [Karl] Rahner [Catholic] to make the Trinity not only the central doctrine of the Christian faith but also the structural principal of Christian theology."[23] Phan then

---

19. Buckley and Yeago, *Knowing the Triune God*, 5, 9.

20. See Buckley and Yeago, *Knowing the Triune* God, 1–20, for more reflections on their project and the contemporary context.

21. *JDDJ*, no. 15.

22. Phan, "Preface," xiii.

23. Phan, "Developments," 1, 11.

proceeds to offer "a theological map to help readers to identify the main issues, tenets, and directions in contemporary trinitarian theology."[24]

In her essay in this volume entitled "Trinity, Christology and Pneumatology," Anne Hunt takes a deeper look at the relationships of the persons of the Trinity. In examining the Scriptural teaching, she concludes: "The Spirit's mission is to mediate the presence of the risen Christ, to interiorize the redemption wrought by Christ, and to animate the ecclesial structures established by Christ." She argues that the Son and Spirit cannot be understood except in relationship with one another.[25] "Ultimately, the Spirit's mission is the incorporation of all humanity, and indeed the whole cosmos, in Christ, and through Christ to the Father (1 Cor 1:5–28; Eph 1:10; Col 1:19–20)."[26] Beside the biblical witness is the liturgical witness "which indicates that Christian worship from very early times is also fashioned along distinctly triadic lines."[27]

Later in her essay, Hunt discusses recent "*Economia* fashioned theologies." She says that these approaches often yield "a socially conceived Trinity, often designated as 'the social model' of the Trinity. With a strong emphasis on the relational and social aspects of personhood, this approach has proved persuasive and appealing in the contemporary milieu."[28] She cites Jurgen Moltmann (Lutheran), John Zizioulas (Orthodox), and Catherine LaCugna (Catholic) as three of the major figures who have used this model.

In the final essay in Phan's volume, Dale T. Irvin considers "The Trinity and Socio-Political ethics" in depth. Being made in God's image "means that human beings are made to be in communion."[29] Irvin goes on to quote Thomas Hopko to the effect that

> human beings . . . are rather like their Creator, made to be persons in community, distinct hypostases in an identity of nature, called to be a perfect—and, according to [Saint] Gregory of Nyssa, even

24. Phan, "Systematic Issues," 13–29. For reflections on the Holy Spirit, see pp. 20–24. See Farrelly, *The Trinity*, 1–29, for another overview of significant contributors to the contemporary discussion.

25. Hunt, "Trinity," 368.

26. Hunt, "Trinity," 367.

27. Hunt, "Trinity," 368. We see here an emphasis on community and communal worship also mentioned in the quotes drawn from the Evangelical-Catholic text above. Chapter 10 will offer further reflections on the Eucharist. Ecumenical ethics is communal as well as individual.

28. Hunt, "Trinity," 375.

29. Irvin, "Trinity," 399.

more perfect—union of being and action in fulfillment of all virtues, the greatest of which is love.[30]

Irvin sees trinitarian ethics as also needing to be ecclesial ethics. He contends that Christians have enough in common that we can draw some general conclusions about trinitarian life and social life in the church. After considering several contemporary questions, Irvin concludes his essay by saying "Thus one finds the ultimate social and political meaning of the Trinity not in itself alone but in its relation to humanity and the whole creation."[31] One might say Christian Social Ethics can be rooted deeply in Trinitarian communion.

Salesian Theology and Spirituality—The Human Person as Image of the Trinity

In the introduction we noted that this text will follow the teaching and spirituality of Saint Francis de Sales. There are a large variety of schools of spirituality that have developed over the two millennia of Christian history.[32] We contend that morality and spirituality are intricately linked. Once a person come to follow Christ, in whatever way that occurs, he or she is on a lifetime spiritual journey that includes the Christian ethics and moral decision making we are discussing.

The "Salesian spirituality" of Francis de Sales, Jane de Chantal, Don Bosco (1815–88), and many others is an important school of Catholic spirituality and theology rooted in the Trinity with significant pastoral and ecumenical overtones. DeSales's gentle, respectful approach to Calvinists was criticized by Catholics in his time but may have been an early sign of the Spirit's guidance toward reconciliation. Francis de Sales was an expert pastor and spiritual director.

DeSales views the human person as made in the image of the Trinity. In one of his early sermons, "Francis gave expression to his belief in the trinitarian structure of God's creative act."[33] Lewis Fiorelli summarizes by saying that "God as Triune is the author of both creation and re-creation.

---

30. Irvin, "Trinity," 400.

31. Irvin, "Trinity," 410.

32. For a concise overview see Farrelly, "Holy Spirit," 501–2. For detailed texts, see the volumes in the Classics of Western Spirituality Series published by Paulist Press.

33. Fiorelli, "Salesian Understanding," 490.

Further, the locus of this divine trinitarian activity is material creation in general and humankind."[34]

DeSales does not dwell on the role of the Father other than to indicate that God empowers creation and re-creation. Francis stresses the role of Christ and the Spirit. It is notable that Francis de Sales adopts the view of the Franciscan Duns Scotus (c. 1266–1308) on the coming of Christ to complete creation. Christ

> is also the reason for creation. Thus, one element of Salesian Anthropology is certainly the Christocentricity of the human person. A creature and prescinding from his subsequent need for a Savior, the human person has an orientation to Jesus Christ from the beginning. . . . We are made in light of Christ and for Francis de Sales "Christ's coming is not first for man's redemption, but for creation's completion."[35]

For DeSales, humans are directed to others. We are made to be loving. In loving others, we become most fully ourselves. Ultimately, we come to the source of our love who is God. This is an anthropology "in which ecstatic love constitutes the image and resemblance in us of the Triune God . . . this love is 'the law of the universe.'"[36]

We also might note that while, as mentioned above, relationships in the Trinity are a major emphasis in contemporary theology, a form of this emphasis on relationships can be seen in Salesian teaching five hundred years ago. There is a richness, a diversity, and a continuity in Christian theology through the centuries.

The Role of the Spirit in Ecumenism

Though the Spirit has been guiding the ecumenical movement since its beginning, and the presence of the Spirit is a common experience for many Christians these days, a focus on the Holy Spirit is a recent phenomenon in the Movement. The ecumenical movement only gradually moved to

---

34. Fiorelli, "Salesian Understanding," 492.

35. Fiorelli, "Salesian Understanding," 493, citing Richard John McKenna. For a short text on Duns Scotus, see Simpson, "Have You Tried Scotus?," 12–15. For a more detailed presentation, see Ward, "Voluntarism," 37–43.

36. Fiorelli, "Salesian Understanding," 494. In chapter 7 we will discuss virtue as an ecumenical ethic and love as the central virtue.

consider the role of the Holy Spirit. A new emphasis on the Spirit began for the members of the World Council of Churches in the 1950s.

Konrad Raiser, then General Secretary of the World Council of Churches, in his 2002 article "Holy Spirit in Ecumenical Thought," traces this new emphasis in detail. Raiser concludes that a coherent doctrine of the Spirit has not yet emerged. He quotes the (1991) Canberra World Council of Churches Assembly Statement: "The Holy Spirit cannot be understood apart from the life of the Holy Trinity. . . . The Spirit is the Power of God, energizing the people of God, corporately and individually, to fulfill their ministry."[37] An emphasis on the Holy Spirit and on spiritual ecumenism is now characteristic of the Movement.[38]

In Richard Lennan and Nancy Pineda-Madrid's recent volume on the Holy Spirit there is an important article by Andrea Vicini on the Holy Spirit and moral theology—a major topic of our study.[39] Vicini begins by saying: "The Holy Spirit is at the heart of the moral life and empowers persons and communities to discern, judge, decide and act by promoting just relationships as well as personal and social flourishing."[40] He goes on to quote a distinguished Protestant moralist who, writing in the pre-Vatican II period, decried the absence of consideration of the relationship of the Holy Spirit to moral theology.[41]

Vicini notes that "In moral life, the Spirit forms and informs one's conscience" and, quoting an evangelical author, "contributes to the 'enrichment and expansion of our moral subjectivity' by entering the hearts of people and empowering 'the ways we function cognitively, volitionally, and affectively.' [Moreover,] the Spirit is present volitionally as the power of conviction in our decision making."[42]

There are many more excellent points in this short article. We would note two further insights. The first is the connection of the Holy Spirit to our emotional lives.

---

37. Raiser, "Holy Spirit," 540. His key points are mentioned in more detail in Crossin, "Moving into the Ecumenical Future," 154.

38. See Kasper, *A Handbook of Spiritual Ecumenism*.

39. This volume from the faculty of the Boston College School of Theology and Ministry, *The Holy Spirit*, shows the breadth of topics and scholarship now available.

40. Vicini, "Empowered," 162.

41. Vicini, "Empowered," 162.

42. Vicini, "Empowered," 163

> Both in the cases of individuals and communities, how we live ethically could benefit from exploring how the Holy Spirit reaches out to human beings by graciously illuminating their emotions, by strengthening or purifying people's emotional lives, or by leading to conversion or reform.[43]

Vicini goes on to indicate how emotions are important for moral development and moral discernment.

The second important point is that emotions are integral—not external—to moral decision making. This is a significant change to previous ways of thinking.

> The importance of emotions in moral discernment, decision making, ethical judgments, and in performing right actions is strengthened by the current understanding of the relation between emotions and rationality, where emotions are considered integral to our reason. Together with many philosophers, theologians, psychologists, and neuroscientists, the philosopher Martha Nussbaum argues that emotions have cognitive content, an intelligence of their own. Thomas Dixon agrees: "The standard view now is that emotions are cognitive states which constitute intelligent appraisals of the world. They are neither mere feelings, nor obstacles to reason."[44]

Thus, we must learn to consider that our rationality and our emotions are deeply connected and not separate—as the quote above mentions. We might prayerfully explore the cultural, familial, and historical formation of our rational and emotional responses. Some of these deeply rooted responses are subconscious. We do well to pray for the guidance of the Holy Spirit and to seek the help of spiritual friends as we seek to become more aware of the roots of our moral decision making.

Concluding Reflections

This chapter presents foundations for the work to follow. We began with a listing of personal experiences of the Holy Spirit. We continued by considering the rise of the international Pentecostal/Charismatic movement(s) with its emphasis not only on the personal experience of the Spirit, but also on the gifts/charisms given by the Spirit. We followed this section by

43. Vicini, "Empowered," 163.
44. Vicini, "Empowered," 167.

considering the importance of pastoral ministry. After some consideration of the Holy Spirit in the context of the Trinity, we mentioned the Salesian view of the human person made in God's image—as made for loving. We concluded with some reflections on the role of the Spirit in ecumenism.

We began this work with an emphasis on the guidance and gifts of the Holy Spirit, on the importance of pastoral ministry, and on the spiritual roots of our ecumenical ethics. We should note that we did not begin with a philosophical analysis. Our approach begins with experiences and moves to the general.

We laid some groundwork in this chapter for building a common ethical paradigm:

a. The emphasis on the guidance of the Spirit.

b. The human person as being in the image of the Trinity and thus made for relationships.

c. The importance of spiritual gifts: certain Christians have the ability to understand moral issues in their complexity.

d. A fourth foundational element is an emphasis on emotion and affect. The Spirit can speak to us through our feelings such as inner joy or sorrow. Modern sciences consider the physical and psychological connections of human emotions and reason. They are not separate.

As we conclude this initial chapter, we do well to recall the Lutheran-Catholic *Joint Declaration*, no. 15. God acts first. We rely on the divine love and mercy that come to us through Christ in the power of the Spirit. We turn now to the pastoral/spiritual life where we ask to be guided by the Spirit in our discernments.

2

Pastoral Ministry and Discernment

Two important elements for building (a) significant ecumenical moral paradigm(s) are reflection on pastoral encounters and discernment of the voice of the Holy Spirit. In this chapter we will offer a few reflections on pastoral accompaniment and consider criteria for individual and communal discernment.

Accompaniment and Dialogue

At a meeting of theologians from the Mediterranean Pope Francis said in part:

> Both movements are necessary and complementary: a bottom-up movement that can dialogue, with an attitude of listening and discernment, with every human and historical stance, taking into account the breadth of what it means to be human; and a top-down movement—where "the top" is that of Jesus lifted up on the cross.

Pope Francis see the pastoral experience as a theological source.[1] Theologians have the task of encouraging anew the encounter of cultures with the sources of Revelation and tradition.

Dialogue is more about listening than talking. As we listen, we can learn much more about the person or persons we are walking with. Our

---

1. See Faggioli, "Ecclesiology," 121–28; Borghesi, *The Mind of Pope Francis*, 44–55.

cultural backgrounds, even if we grew up in the same country, can be radically different. In listening and asking a few questions, we can learn a great deal about others' lives and their cultural/spiritual roots.

By listening first rather than speaking, we can avoid making mistakes based on a lack of understanding of a person's background and experience. More importantly, my early pastoral experience was that what I first heard was not the deeper reality within the person. As we built mutual confidence, people often shared some of their weaknesses rather than just their positive public *persona*. My view of them changed significantly as we shared more deeply.

By listening to and engaging others we also can begin to learn what they are capable of understanding and doing at the present time. For example, does a person or group have enough moral understanding to know how their actions might impact others? Has an individual enough empathy to put him or herself in the place of another? There are levels of moral development. Both intellectual and emotional factors are involved in moral decision making and acting.[2] Wisdom lies in asking people to do things they are capable of understanding and doing.

People whom we accompany also can and should challenge those of us who minister. Ministers do not have all the answers and sometimes we need things pointed out to us. All of us can use the opportunity to practice a little humility.

What we are listening for is not agreement but the voice of the Holy Spirit coming to us through others. We cannot limit the Spirit's speaking to people we like or who agree with us. Sometimes it is the least likely person who speaks God's word as we walk together and converse. Often, we only realize that God was speaking later when we are mulling over or praying over our conversation.

Such irony is not absent in God's call to us. The recent decades of the crisis over pedophilia have humiliated Catholic clergy and laity alike. These humiliations have not been limited to Catholics as this crisis has touched other Christians as well. The need for healing of all those affected is widespread. This healing process promises to play out over many years. These humiliations have sometimes opened us to listen more attentively to others, especially our honest critics.

Marcus Mescher in his recent book *The Ethics of Encounter: Christian Neighbor Love as a Practice of Solidarity* moves us forward in proposing

2. See Gibbs, *Moral Development and Reality*, 1–18.

"how a culture of encounter can become a step along the way toward building a culture of solidarity."[3] He offers a comprehensive, well-documented
discussion of accompaniment and its implications. He contends that an
ethics of encounter involves

> a framework for practicing encounter that affirms innate and equal
> human dignity, practices neighbor love, heals social divisions, and
> fosters social trust through mutual respect and responsibility. I en-
> vision this as a dynamic and diverse process with steps advancing
> from encountering others, to accompanying others, to meaning-
> ful exchange with others, to cultivating the kind of rapport and
> tenderness that animate an embrace of others, thus building an
> inclusive belonging and accountability that generates solidarity.[4]

Mescher is not naive about the difficulties one can meet as one encounters others and builds relationships. He is candid and offers processes
that might mitigate problems. He believes that the obstacles can be in us
or in the neighbor. He also believes that God is present in every encounter
even a negative one.[5]

I believe that in developing an ecumenical ethical paradigm to provide a framework for considering new moral issues and revisiting older
ones, we also will be contributing to building common Christian culture(s)
that bring people together in mutual respect.

Discernment: Initial Reflections

As we accompany other individuals and groups and minister to them, we
seek the guidance of the Holy Spirit.[6] Pope Francis and many others refer
to engaging in discernment about how best to serve those with whom we
are walking.[7] This process focuses on the individual or on the group and
the specifics of relationships, knowledge, motivation, thoughts, and feelings that make the person(s) unique. I would note that this starting point
leads to a greater emphasis on individual differences, even among people

---

3. Mescher, *Ethics*, xviii.

4. Mescher, *Ethics*, xviii.

5. Mescher, *Ethics*, 186.

6. For some helpful, concise reflections on the Holy Spirit, see biblical scholar Montague, *Holy Spirit*.

7. Francis, *Gaudete et exsultate*, nos. 166–77.

of similar backgrounds, and less emphasis on generalities about human nature or human goals that one sees with starting points in philosophy,

My intention is to emphasize certain salient aspects of discernment drawn from Saint Francis de Sales and related authors that may be helpful to those in ministry.[8] I will also add a few reflections on group discernment.

I should recall that not only are there different schools of thought on discerning God's will but there are also efforts to develop new thinking about discernment. Edward Collins Vacek, SJ, in "Discernment within a Mutual Love Relationship with God: A New Theological Foundation" offers some stimulating contemporary reflections. He contends:

> Methods of discernment are numerous and fallible. Spiritual writers depict discerners as passively receiving God's will or discovering God's predetermined plan. As an alternative, this article proposes that an illuminating, mutual love relationship with God requires humans to codetermine God's will for themselves and others. They respond to the Spirit who frees and leads by attraction.[9]

I should note that discerning God's will is a process that engages human freedom and does not achieve absolute but rather relative certainty. Our discernment is in service to others as we walk with them.

We continue by considering Andre Brouillette's reflections on "Discerning the Action of God." He considers both Teresa of Avila and Ignatius Loyola in his concise essay. Francis de Sales not only was educated by Jesuits and thus familiar with Saint Ignatius but also drew on the spiritual insights of Saint Teresa in his *Treatise on the Love of God.*

Citing Ignatius, Brouillette mentions that "The nondiscursive language of the Spirit pertains to the affective realm, we are eminently touched by the Spirit." He goes on to indicate that given the challenge of hearing the word of the Spirit amidst daily busyness, "Ignatius developed a grammar of the language of the Spirit. The two basic signs of that grammar are consolation and desolation. Consolation . . . is akin to Paul's fruits of the Spirit: inner peace, joy, and love [Gal 5:22–23]. Desolation . . . entails sadness, dryness, a feeling of estrangement from God, lack of faith, hope and charity."[10] One

---

8. For a deeper exposition, see my chapter on "Moral Discernment" in Crossin, *Walking in Virtue,* 61–74; Crossin, "What Does God Want Us to Do?," 146–49; Therese, "Salesian Discernment," 201–12.

9. Vacek, "Discernment," 683–710.

10. Brouillette, "Discerning the Action," 109–11. Saint Teresa believes that the choice of a spiritual director is most important (115).

can look at one's consolations and desolations in one's daily *examen* and in regular conversations with a spiritual director.

A significant element in Brouillette's presentation on Saint Teresa is on the "dynamics of the Spirit." These

> can be uncovered in the testimonial teaching of Teresa of Avila as a threefold movement of disjunction, emptying/incarnation, and inspiration. This movement is also confirmed in an essential locus: peace. . . . The final moment of this dynamic is inspiration; the Spirit inspires guiding toward action.[11]

Desolation/Consolation, inner peace, following the inspiration of the Spirit, action for the good as inspired, and the importance of spiritual direction are all elements in Francis de Sales' reflections on discernment. The influence of Saints Ignatius and Teresa are very evident in Francis de Sales.

Brouillette also mentions the noted French Dominican theologian Yves Congar and Congar's trilogy of books on the Holy Spirit. Congar groups the criteria for discernment under three dimensions: the objective, the subjective and the communal.

- Objective discernment might include—as appropriate—doctrinal elements of the church.

- One's Subjective experience—the main focus in personal discernment—involves many factors some of which we have already mentioned.

- Communal discernment invites all to listen for the Spirit, to read the "signs of the times"; to listen to members knowledgeable in spirituality and expert in other aspects of the discernment; and to decide.[12]

Salesian Spirituality

Saint Francis de Sales is most noted as the author of the *Introduction to the Devout Life* (1608). In DeSales' lifetime this spiritual classic was valued by Anglicans as well as Catholics. It is still published today.[13] Part III of

11. Brouillette, "Discerning the Action," 112–13.

12. Brouillette, "Discerning the Action," 114. See Congar, *I Believe in the Holy Spirit*, 182–83.

13. See John K. Ryan's translation of DeSales' *Introduction to the Devout Life*. Ryan is quite attentive to the actual text.

the *Introduction* discusses the "little virtues" for daily living including humility, patience and gentleness with self and others. These are key virtues for ecumenical dialogue which includes respect for others—even for one's opponents.[14] I would note again that one's Christian colleague, even in a moment of disagreement, can be speaking God's word.

DeSales was named a Doctor of the Church by Pope Pius IX in 1877. His theology is rooted in Scripture. In his theology we see a synthesis of Bonaventure, Scotus, Teresa of Avila, Augustine, Aquinas, and many other thinkers.[15] His wide-ranging synthesis points to the richness of the Christian theological traditions. It also points to the fact that such new syntheses are acceptable in the emerging world church.

There are many different approaches and schools of thought that have develop in the last two thousand years. As Christian thinking moves from the hyperclarity and conflict of the post-Reformation period to a more nuanced historical view of the rich diversity and differences of theological thought and schools of thought, DeSales's example reminds us that ecumenical agreement needs to be on basics and not on the preferences or presuppositions of the members of one or another theological school.

Thomas Donlon's ongoing research confirms and elaborates on Congar's observation that Francis de Sales was the Reformation era Catholic leader most likely to be picked to preach at a contemporary prayer service for Christian Unity.[16] Donlon observes:

> Using the concept of *douceur* or gentleness, Francois de Sales fervently critiqued the aggressive, fearful piety prevalent among French Catholics in the sixteenth and seventeenth centuries, exhorting the faithful to a hopeful, merciful, and humble imitation of Christ. This essay will examine the Salesian reform of militant Catholicism, detailing how *Francois* embodied and promoted gentleness first in missionary work, second in the sacrament of penance and spiritual direction, and finally in his approach to asceticism.[17]

Francis de Sales, as the reforming Catholic bishop of Geneva headquartered in Annecy in the Kingdom of Savoy, emphasized pastoral care. He

14. For a very good overview of Salesian Spirituality, see Francis de Sales and Jane de Chantal, *Letters of Spiritual Direction*, 9–90. For more on gentleness, see pp. 63–65.

15. See Bowden, "*Ma tres chere fille*," 71–82. For a popular presentation, see Simpson, "Have You Tried Scotus?," 12–15.

16. Congar, "St. Francis de Sales Today," 9.

17. Donlon, "Oasis of Gentleness," 91. See more in Donlon, *The Reform of Zeal*.

personally visited hundreds of parishes in his far-flung diocese. Some were so inaccessible in the mountains that they had not seen their bishop in a century or more! DeSales wrote a short instruction on preaching for priests in his early days as bishop. He was widely sought as a spiritual director.

Salesian Discernment

Having presented some insights into discernment and action drawn from two well-known Catholic saints, and the preeminent theologian at the Second Vatican Council, let me turn now to a few insights drawn from Francis de Sales and some personal comments.[18]

DeSales reflections on discernment need to be approached in the context of regular personal prayer and reflection on the Scriptures. The parables of Jesus, for example, can shape our way of looking at life situations. We can ask ourselves if we are "the priest who walked by" in the parable of the Good Samaritan or the uncomprehending disciples who met Jesus on the Road to Emmaus—and only eventually recognized him. The deep background for discernment is personal and communal prayer and Christian formation.

Part of our discernment process is sharing things with spiritual friends.[19] In Salesian thinking, the spiritual director mentioned earlier is one type of spiritual friend. Spiritual friends are men and women who share about the spiritual journey and have one another's spiritual well-being at heart. These friends are usually not numerous and are sent by God. We can seek their wise counsel as we make our decisions about pastoral care.

In the context of accompanying others and seeking to minister to them in an effective way, we might seek the counsel of friends who have pastoral experience. A critical aspect of serving others is respecting the uniqueness of each person—not just seeing a person as part of a group—and seeking to serve her/him/them in ways that are best in the present moment. Francis de Sales is well-known for saying "we must live in the present moment."[20] We have to minister to those we walk with in the present moment given the real

18. These days, Catholic, Orthodox, and Protestant spiritual and theological writers have studied together and/or read one another's writings. The clear lines of demarcation that once existed are now cloudy and often nonexistent.

19. Spiritual Friendship will also be discussed in chapter 4 below.

20. See Francis de Sales and Jane de Chantal, *Letters of Spiritual Direction*, 112.

context and the strengths, weaknesses, insights, and blind-spots of those we are accompanying—and of ourselves.

One aspect of this accompaniment is *healing*. Every person has negative past experiences, sins, and fears. No one is without burdens. Part of accompaniment is to be a listening and loving presence that facilitates healing. The virtue of *gentleness*, of respect for the person made in the image of God, comes into play. Listening with gentleness and compassion and without quick judgments can be of great importance.

For someone to speak aloud about a trauma or difficulty buried deep within them to an accepting and merciful person can be very healing. "Speaking it aloud" can also help the speaker to see him/herself more clearly.

Another virtue that comes into play in accompaniment is *patience*. Healing—and perhaps reconciliation—will only come in God's time and cannot be forced. Regularly keeping others in prayer and speaking words of encouragement are appropriate. God's timing can be mysterious to those of us in ministry. "Holy indifference" is a factor in spiritual discernment. Eventually we must give everything over to God.

Giving our discernment to God requires a certain amount of *humility*. Francis de Sales discusses humility in his *Introduction*. He offers quite practical suggestions. His discussion moves from "Outward Humility to Deeper Inner Humility to Loving Our Abjections." For Francis de Sales:

- Humility flows from *gratitude* for the gifts we have been given.

- Humility wishes to conceal itself.

- Humility embraces our "abjections" especially those not chosen.

- And Humility includes sincerity, candor, and realism.[21]

In entering a discernment process, practicing the virtues, considering varied courses of action, learning to "let go," and then deciding, we often come to a place of inner peace and joy. These are signs of the presence of the Spirit. From my experience, I would say that the peace and joy are usually most evident as the resolution of what should be done is near.

21. This summary and other points that follow are found in Crossin, "A Meditation on Humility," 181–91.

Communal Discernment

My experience of discernment by communities is not as extensive as my walking with others who are engaging in personal discernment.[22] I recently have listed and reflected on some of the most important elements I have experienced in communal discernment and need not repeat these details here.[23] Rather I will note two key elements of communal discernment. The first is detailed preparation. In the appendix to this volume, I have offered suggestions for the detailed preparation for a task group that would be discerning an ecumenical moral paradigm. The second key element is attention to the presentations of the members of the discerning group.

Personal Reflections

I should mention that there is considerable overlap in the moral literature in the meaning and use of the terms prudence, conscience, and discernment. This is not to say that these terms have exactly the same meaning.[24] The word discernment has a more subjective overtone to it. None of these terms, though they have been part of the Christian moral tradition for centuries, received a central emphasis in Catholic moral theologizing in the decades before the Second Vatican Council.

Discernment needs to be accomplished in a reasonable time. We can fall out of touch with a person or group if we take too long. Good discernment is practical about time and about other reality-making factors such as a place to meet, the resources available, and the like.

A good discernment considers the opportune timing of events and the availability of people. One discerning pastor I know had some of his baptismal preparation sessions early in the morning or later in the evening so that parishioners who rode the bus or worked late hours would be able to attend.

As one embraces discernment more fully it can take place daily. We can eventually get to that point on the spiritual journey where we are

22. There is literature on discernment by congregations accessible on the internet. For a very interesting reflection on communal "Discernment of Spirits," see the International Catholic-Pentecostal Dialogue, "Do Not Quench the Spirit," nos. 73–90.

23. See Crossin, "Will Christian Unity Come Sooner?," 19–20.

24. See chapter 4 for a discussion of prudence and chapter 10 for more on conscience.

mindful many times a day of the divine presence and are regularly seeking divine guidance.

This book is encouraging further discernment together by Christian communities on how to establish specific moral teaching.

- What are the foundations for a teaching in pastoral experience, spirituality, and Scripture?

- Furthermore, what are the central elements agreed on by Christians?

- What is/are the paradigm(s) for such decision making?

- What are the processes for reaching conclusions?

- What issues can entertain a spectrum of views or different schools of thought?

- How are practical applications made in real, sometimes unusual, situations?

A question of relevance is whether discernment should become an integral part of Christian religious instruction. If there were to be a differentiated consensus on moral teaching as there was on the doctrine of justification in the 1999 *JDDJ*, would training in discerning the guidance of the Spirit both individually and communally be necessary? And what virtues and practices are needed to move discernment from being a practice for ministers and for devout laity to being an essential dimension of the moral life for all Christians?

3

Biblical Ethics

LUCAS CHAN, SJ, WAS an eminent Catholic authority on biblical ethics in the last decade in the United States.[1] He noted:

> For centuries, the use of Scripture in Christian ethics has differentiated Protestants from Catholics. The Reformers turned to Scripture as the primary source of moral wisdom; Catholics reiterate, instead, their dependency on tradition. The Second Vatican Council, however, admonished Catholic moral theologians to turn to Scripture: "Special care should be given to the perfecting of moral theology. Its scientific presentation should draw more fully on the teaching of Holy Scripture."[2]

Jared Wicks, SJ, in his text *Investigating Vatican II: Its Theologians, Ecumenical Turn and Biblical Commitment* concludes that *Dei verbum* [Dogmatic Constitution on Divine Revelation] points Catholics toward daily spiritual nourishment from *lectio divina* of scripture.[3] Not only professional ethicists but all Christians are to root their life and prayer in the Scriptures. Ecumenical ethics certainly will need to ground itself in prayer and biblical teaching. The guidance of the Spirit through the inspired word

---

1. Father Chan's sudden death in mid-life was a great loss to Christian unity. I will draw several significant points from Chan's publications, but my presentations will be far from capturing his total contribution.

2. Chan, *The Ten Commandments*, ix.

3. Wicks, *Investigating Vatican II*, 257.

of Scripture is of utmost importance. Protestants, Orthodox, and Catholics now have a common biblical foundation for their personal moral reflection and communal life.

In this chapter, we begin by reviewing some history of the use of the Bible in Christian theology. It is important to note that the teaching of Scripture was central in the ancient church and that the critical use of then–contemporary philosophy was taking place early on. It also was noted early in Christian history that Scripture has a depth of meaning. In moving forward to the contemporary situation, we stress the importance of Judaism with its ongoing wrestling with the Scripture and the work of Lucas Chan on integrating Scriptural teaching with contemporary ethical concerns. These many emphases lay groundwork for our contention that the core elements for an ecumenical paradigm will come from the Scriptures.

Historical Glimpses

The mandate to prioritize the Scriptures is clear. The common history of Christians dating back to the beginning focuses on the Scriptures. Charles H. Cosgrove offers a concise overview of this focus in his "Scripture in Ethics: A History." Two points he makes are of special significance:

> The Fathers developed the concept of the inspiration of Scripture by the Holy Spirit, and by the fourth century the basic contours of the canon were established. They also assumed that Scripture contains levels of meaning beyond the ordinary meaning of its words.
>
> Conceiving moral existence in terms of virtues and vices was a traditional approach, going back to the fathers and especially to Augustine, who derived the theological virtues [faith, hope and love] from Scripture (with 1 Cor 13:13 providing the hermeneutical key) and the natural virtues from the Greco-Roman philosophical tradition as mediated through Christian reflection.[4]

One of the earliest authors to develop a systematic approach to theology was Irenaeus of Lyons (c. 130–c. 202). . He lived in the latter half of the second century and along with Clement of Alexandria (c. 150–215) and Tertullian (c. 150/160—220/240) is considered a major figure of that time.[5] His *Against the Heresies* is one of the first works of systematic theology. Yet

4. Cosgrove, "Scripture in Ethics," 16, 18.

5. Gonzalez, *History*, 76.

this work was more exegesis of Scripture than abstract discussion.[6] Scripture dominated though philosophical thought Christianized was often integrated with it as systematic theology developed.

Gregory W. Dawes in his "The Interpretation of the Bible" gives an overview of biblical interpretation from the patristic period to today's postmodern approaches. A major insight is his contention that "the Bible is always interpreted, even when it is read by an unsophisticated reader who would never think of being an interpreter."[7]

In this context I should mention that the editors of Francis de Sales and Jane de Chantal, *Letters of Spiritual Direction*, note:

> In a manner remarkable for a Counter-Reformation bishop, Francis de Sales exudes a familiarity with the stories, the sense and indeed the text of the Bible. He spontaneously used scriptural examples and phrases, as he said, "not always to explain them, but to explain myself by means of them." If this was true of his published work, it is even more evident in his letters.[8]

This is not the practice of contemporary biblical scholarship, but DeSales' approach resonates with preachers even today. Furthermore, he was attentive to the humanist biblical hermeneutics of his time which was an advance over previous eras. DeSales' emphasis was more on the spiritual and mystical meaning of Scripture.[9] More importantly, we see that his

---

6. See Parvis, "Who Was Irenaeus?," 18.

7. Dawes, "The Interpretations of the Bible," 16. I should note that Catholic teaching found in the Pontifical Biblical Commission's 1993 document "The Interpretation of the Bible in the Church" raises questions about "Fundamentalist Interpretation." The Commission members note some limited strengths of this approach but consider it very faulted as it "refuses to take into account the historical character of biblical revelation." The approach is a version of "literalism" to the exclusion of deeper insights into the biblical text. It can offer people "pious but illusory" interpretations instead of indicating that the "Bible does not necessarily contain an immediate answer to each and every problem" (73, 75). Benedict XVI, *The Word of the Lord*, 69–70, affirmed this position.

8. Francis de Sales and Jane de Chantal, *Letters of Spiritual Direction*, 91.

9. See McGoldrick, "The Living Word," esp. 97 where McGoldrick concludes: Francis de Sales' "new mysticism drew from the language of Scripture's imagery, in stories, history, poetry and the life of Jesus, but it also found its own language. His biblical hermeneutic reflected his unique contribution as a pastor and Christian humanist, who proclaimed that God could be known by the common man and woman with a devotion equal to those in traditional religious life. Tying all to the imagery of Scripture, de Sales both made the universal message understandable in the age of images and emblems, but it also saved his new mysticism from rancorous criticism."

mind was shaped by the biblical teaching as was encouraged by the Second Vatican Council.

In his "Foreword" to Lucas Chan's book, *Biblical Ethics in the 21ˢᵗ Century*, James F. Keenan, SJ, offers a concise overview of Catholic Moral Theology since the twelfth century. In summary he says, "Our history shows us that the moral theology of Roman Catholics . . . did not depend much on the Bible."[10] He also traces how this changed—beginning with a few authors who were writing before the Second Vatican Council and culminating in the work of William Spohn and his book, *Go and Do Likewise: Jesus and Ethics* in 1999.

As noted above, the Second Vatican Council encouraged Scripture study and a renewal of moral theology rooted in Scripture. A good overview of Catholic Church documents since the Council is found in Ronald J. Witherup, PSS, "The Bible in the Life of the Church" where he offers an exposition and analysis. A key point for our discussions is that the Second Vatican Council saw Scripture and tradition as going together and forming "one sacred deposit of the word of God."[11] Tradition is dynamic with insights into the holy word growing over time.[12]

Richard J. Clifford, SJ, and Thomas D. Stegman, SJ, offer some interesting present–day reflections in their article on "The Christian Bible." They see an overall unity to all seventy-three books of the Bible in the three exodus moments—the exodus from Egypt, the exodus from Babylon, and the exodus of the life and ministry of Jesus culminating in his death and

10. Keenan, "Foreword," vii. For an exposition in greater detail, see Keenan, *A History*, chs. 1–5.

11. Second Vatican Council, *Dei verbum*, no. 10.

12. Witherup, "The Bible in the Life," 16–17. For more comments on the relationship of Scripture and Tradition, see Tavard, "Tradition." Tavard offers a historical overview and lists some "Contemporary Debates." Orthodox theologian and bishop Kallistos Ware has a different approach in his "Tradition and Traditions," 1144. He first considers the New Testament; he then reflects on the Early Church concluding that "For patristic authors in general . . . tradition does not constitute a supplementary source of information about Christ alongside scripture, but it denotes simply the manner in which scripture is interpreted and lived by successive generations within the church;" he reviews the Reformation debate and recent changes, for example, in Catholicism at Vatican II; and he sees a developing ecumenical convergence. Significantly, Ware mentions that men and women saints, not just bishops, transmit tradition. Raymond Brown's balanced position is that "'tension' can exist between the church's teaching and the biblical data that is appealed to in support of it . . . [but] I would not accept the opposite extreme which allows the literal meaning and the church interpretation to be contradictory in the strict sense." Senior, *Raymond E. Brown*, 71.

resurrection. The apocalyptic expectations of Jesus' time were fulfilled by him in an unexpected way. Each exodus incorporates the previous one. "The full realization of the kingdom lies in the future."[13] There is a future orientation to the gospel message which an ecumenical ethics should emphasize.

Jewish Background

Clifford and Stegman with their three exodus moments point to the unity of the Scriptures. One cannot really understand Jesus and the New Testament without the Jewish background. In commentaries since the Second Vatican Council, scholars often refer to the Jewish Scriptures to understand the gospel text. "We now see it as our task to bring these two ways of re-reading the biblical texts—the Christian Way and the Jewish Way—into dialogue with one another, if we are to understand God's will and his word aright."[14] For example, Daniel J. Harrington, SJ, in his commentary on the Sermon on the Mount continually refers to the Old Testament texts related to the Sermon.[15]

Noted German biblical scholar Gerhard Lohfink in his *Is This All There Is? On Resurrection and Eternal Life* remarks that Israel's sober mindedness and worldliness keeps Christians grounded in the real material world where we live. One Christian manifestation of this grounding is receiving ashes at the beginning of Lent. We "are nothing but dust—the dust of dead stars."

Lohfink goes further with this important observation:

> The way in which the Old Testament people of God slowly found its path to faith in an eternal life with God, through steady distancing from the religions of its surrounding world, was complex. If we contemplate this history, we shall also see the "outside" of revelation. We sense how revelation really happens: not through dictation from heaven but on the real basis of a people that entrusts itself to God and lets itself be led by God, ceaselessly observing, comparing, criticizing, sifting—at the same time repeatedly investigating its own history and when necessary, seeing it with new eyes. That is the way of revelation. That is the only way that God

13. Clifford and Stegman, "The Christian Bible," 1648.

14. Benedict XVI, as cited in Cunningham, *Seeking Shalom*, 252.

15. Harrington, *Gospel of Matthew*, 76–111. See Clifford, "Changing Christian Interpretations," 509: "The article sketches the first-century situation, looks at subsequent interpretation, and calls on recent Roman Catholic documents to revise old assumptions."

speaks to the world, and in that sense, Christians also believe in the self-revealing, true and only God.[16]

Our understanding of the depth of God's revelation to us is an ongoing process as it was/is for the Jewish people. We will see the divine revelation with "new eyes" as our predecessors did.[17]

Our work on an ecumenical ethic could include reference to Jewish scholars's interpretations of the Christian Bible as, for example, those in the *Jewish Annotated New Testament*. Likewise essays by Jewish scholars on selected topics such as Jonathan Klawans essay on "The Law" in the *Jewish Annotated New Testament* can be helpful.[18]

We could likewise continue to pay attention to the views of Jewish ethicists as we address common moral issues. For example, Alain Thomasset, SJ, in his essay "The Virtue of Hospitality according to the Bible and the Challenge of Migration," cites Rabbi Jonathan Sacks' interpretation of the actions of Abraham in welcoming the three strangers in Genesis 18:1–33.[19]

The Society for Jewish Ethics and the Society for Christian Ethics are having joint annual meetings with the availability of the presentations of both to all in attendance. These efforts can become part of our building positive interrelationships of mutual concern and respect that can enhance and deepen a new and positive narrative.

The Integration of Scripture and Ethics

Our changing emphasis on our relationship with Jewish scholarship leads us into the work of Lucas Chan. He was a major exponent of a deeper integration of contemporary biblical scholarship and Christian ethics. James F. Keenan remarks that Lucas Chan's work in *Biblical Ethics in the 21ˢᵗ Century*[20]

---

16. Lohfink, *Is This All There Is?*, 92. For further reflections on development of doctrine, see chapter 9.

17. See Greenberg, "From Enemy to Partner," 190–95. Rabbi Greenberg argues that the revisioning of Christianity after the Holocaust of its relationship with Judaism especially in *Nostra Aetate* is leading Judaism to its own revisioning. He makes a salient case for new paradigms for mutual understanding.

18. Klawans, "The Law," 515–18.

19. Thomasset, "The Virtue of Hospitality," 37.

20. James F. Keenan finished the "Introduction" to *The Bible and Catholic Theological Ethics* and included comments about Lucas Chan after his sudden death in 2015.

described the developments in the field of biblical ethics since the second edition of [William] Spohn's *What Are They Saying about Scripture and Ethics*. . . . His account was critical and prescriptive. Throughout his book, he argued that biblicists need to attend to the hermeneutical work of moral theologians and moral theologians need to found their hermeneutical work on the exegetical work of biblicists.[21]

Chan was a pioneer in this integrated approach. He analyzed the work of both Catholic and Protestant scholars in the collaborative ecumenical spirit evident since the Second Vatican Council and the initiation of ecumenical dialogues. We will mention only a few of the insights offered in his *Biblical Ethics*. His work is worth a more detailed study than can be accomplished here.[22]

Chan reviews the work of distinguished biblical scholars and then moves on to consider the work of noted moral theologians. He is seeking to garner from these distinguished biblical scholars and moral theologians methodological insights that can "shape the future of Scripture-based ethics."[23]

A few major points that Chan makes in his chapters that follow his "Introduction" to his *Biblical Ethics* deserve mention. He makes note, for example, of the fact that while we seek unified Scriptural themes, we must also respect the diversity found in the Scriptures.[24]

In discussing the work of theological ethicists further, he mentions that "one's ethical framework is crucial to how biblical texts are used and interpreted."[25] This is an important point for us to keep in mind as we develop an ecumenical ethical paradigm. I would affirm that presuppositions can affect the results of moral reflection based on my own experience.

In his review of the work of prominent biblical scholars and Christian ethicists, Chan notes that they tend to stress what they know well—the text or ethical hermeneutics, respectively. Chan sees that a balance between the two is necessary.

---

21. Keenan, "Introduction," 3. By biblical hermeneutics, we mean the study of principles for the interpretation of the Bible.

22. Some of Chan's reflections on biblical hermeneutics can be found in chapter 7.

23. Chan, *Biblical Ethics*, 6.

24. Chan, *Biblical Ethics*, 28.

25. Chan, *Biblical Ethics*, 50.

Chan proceeds to examine in some detail the writings of biblical scholar Richard Burridge and Christian ethicist Allen Verhey. He builds parts of his own hermeneutical proposal on their insights.

Richard Burridge is well-known for viewing the Gospels as biographies or biographical narratives.[26] A key point of his is that while most New Testament ethics focuses on the "rigorous ethical teachings of Jesus" it neglects the fact that "one must set Jesus' ethical teaching within the context of the narrative that portrays his deeds." The starting point for ethics is Jesus. The call is to Christian discipleship.[27]

Chan gives another thoughtful analysis in examining the work of Allen Verhey. He finds Verhey's "understanding of the Sermon on the Mount in Matthew 5–7 . . . gives hints of the kind of ethical approach Verhey has in mind for his own proposal—one that emphasizes character formation and virtues."[28]

Verhey believes that the ethicist must take the biblical teaching seriously and study it in depth. But he also takes the next step out into the biblical world by offering considered opinions on the texts. Verhey tends to emphasize practices and "understands ethics as primarily a matter of communal practice."[29] Scripture is the source of renewal of church life, but Verhey *does allow* for other sources such as "natural science, natural morality, and human experiences" as necessary elements in Christian ethics.[30]

Considering Verhey's endorsement of other sources, let me underline the importance prayer and of communal discernment seeking the guidance of the Holy Spirit. I am suggesting that Christians may need to change their practices of denominational discernment to allow for discernment of God's will with representatives of other Christian traditions. Providentially, the ecumenical relationships exist that would facilitate such common efforts.

The Importance of Virtue Ethics

At the conclusion of the introduction of his work in *Biblical Ethics*, Chan first notes that VE with its emphasis on Christian character has become

---

26. See Burridge, *What Are the Gospels?*
27. Chan, *Biblical Ethics*, 54, 55.
28. Chan, *Biblical Ethics*, 65.
29. Chan, *Biblical Ethics*, 66.
30. Chan, *Biblical Ethics*, 67.

more prominent in recent decades.[31] He goes on to say that "in terms of the narratives and the overall ends of Scripture themselves, we will see that virtue ethics is the most congruent and the most able to bear the weight of interpretation."[32]

Chan goes forward in exploring how virtue ethics is a good and distinctive "Hermeneutical Tool" for the relationship of Scripture to ethics.[33]

Some Recent Developments

In his essay, "Biblical Ethics: 3D,"[34] Chan expands his vision in reviewing some of the recent work from North America and overseas.[35] This essay appears in a book of essays that Chan organized with James Keenan and Renaldo Zacharias.[36] The book consists of contributions from theologians around the globe on diverse moral topics and their relationship to the Bible. This shows the international scope of biblical ethics.

James Keenan summarizes the work of these theologians in saying:

> Zacharias's [concluding] essay is filled with hope and promise. Like the collection itself, it centers on the foundational claims about how the Scriptures can and are being received. Many of these essays are about fundamental biblical claims such as *hesed*, the Decalogue, the kingdom of God, or the new creation, whereas others are about fundamental methods for bridging the texts. . . . Others are instructive in reflecting on how we preach the Scriptures or how we read and receive them.[37]

The collection's authors provide interesting insights. Two examples give a hint of their richness: While conveying moral teaching and moving the will are important, more important for Alain Thomasset is imagination. "Imagination is the mediation between the world of the text and the reader's appropriation."[38] For Aristide Fumagalli, "a fruitful encounter is

---

31. See Crossin, *What Are They Saying about Virtue?*, for an early summary of this trend which is now in full bloom.

32. Chan, *Biblical Ethics*, 7.

33. Chan, *Biblical Ethics*, xvi–xvii.

34. The original version appeared in *Theological Studies* 76 (2015) 112–28.

35. Chan, "Biblical Ethics," 22–27.

36. Chan et al. eds. *The Bible and Catholic Theological Ethics*.

37. Keenan, "Introduction," 12.

38. Thomasset, "The Virtue of Hospitality," 36.

needed between the proclamation of the Christian truth and the welcoming of human liberty." We can do this, using parables as Jesus did, because they activate the listener better than anything else.[39]

Concluding Reflections

The approach outlined above is quite different from the teaching I experienced as a boy. That teaching emphasized following the law and confessing one's sins. The Bible was in the chest in our dining room and contained the family genealogy. We rarely consulted it.

Later as part of my theological studies I read segments of one of the pre-Vatican II moral manuals with their focus on interpreting the ten commandments and on natural law with an occasional "proof text" from the bible. This is far from the writers of the first millennium mentioned above and from the current practice of moral theologians.

In developing a paradigm for a common Christian ethics, we will need to continue this collaboration and integration of the work of biblical scholars and Christian ethicists. The effort will be ongoing because the biblical teaching is so deep and can always be known and lived better. Our need to relate gospel teaching to contemporary situations in various parts of the world will challenge our principles for interpretation [our hermeneutics]. Thus, integration will be ongoing and not static.

Gospel teaching is a vital foundation for ethics and for ministry. Pope Francis, in his Exhortation *Evangelii gaudium* comments:

> Meanwhile, the Gospel tells us constantly to run the risk of a face–to–face encounter with others. . . . True faith in the incarnate Son of God is inseparable from self-giving, from membership in the community, from service, from reconciliation with others. The Son of God, by becoming flesh, summoned us to the revolution of tenderness.[40]

Love is the central virtue of our Christian lives.[41]

---

39. Fumagalli, "Biblical Ethics and the Proclamation of the Gospel," 102
40. Francis, *Evangelii gaudium*, No. 18.
41. See chapters 7 and 8.

4

Personal Relationships in a Relational Universe

THE SCRIPTURES PROVIDE THE strong foundation for communal life and for ecumenical ethics.[1] Lasting relationships have been and are being built between churches and individuals. Now we dialogue with one another and often provide mutual support. Our relationships are being healed.[2] This chapter will concern itself with many aspects of our relationships—with one another in friendship, community, and ministry; with the natural world as understood by modern science; with our grounding in philosophy and theology; and with our history.

Preliminary Observations

In recent years there has been—at least in the United States—a turn inward. The Christian traditions, now experiencing a serious decline in membership, have been looking to their own identity. Overall, this can be quite

---

1. See Ruedi-Weber, "Bible," 108–12. One salient passage mentions that "the testimony given in holy scripture 'affords the primary norm for the church's teaching, worship and life.' This does not mean that all must have the same doctrinal understanding of biblical authority, but it does imply that all are ready to be guided, questioned and corrected by the biblical message in their various doctrinally and culturally conditioned situations" (108).

2. See Crossin, "Building Relationships with Others," 6–7, 9.

beneficial for ecumenism. We cannot continue to have fruitful dialogue unless we have some clarity about our identity.

On the other hand, in this process of seeking identity there can be a tendency to ignore the gifts given to us by other Christian communities.[3] Christian identity needs to be understood more broadly than in the past. Our "boundaries" need to be drawn not narrowly but more comprehensively. The Holy Spirit has been at work in the Christian communities even when they were distant from one another.

Former archbishop of Canterbury and primate of the Church of England, Rowan Williams mentions the possible danger: "Each of us stands in a condition of separateness, clinging to our markers of identity; and these markers of identity readily become defenses and barriers against each other."[4]

Archbishop Williams goes on to say that while each of us maintain his or her basic character and identity, each of us must grow spiritually. Dialogue

> does involve stripping away those habits that allow me to anchor my security in what sets me apart from others. Only so do I become reliant on God alone, and become the agent of his love, not my own good will, moral energy, or spiritual resourcefulness. In this way only do I share in Christ's act—Christ making himself one with humanity, in a process that culminates in his dereliction on the cross and his cry of forsakenness.[5]

Archbishop Williams's remarks remind us that spiritual ecumenism is central to our ecumenical work. We seek to discern the Spirit's work in our midst. We realize that we will have "to let go" of some thoughts and feelings to follow the road the Spirit walks with us.[6]

During the centuries of conflict, we Catholics sought to be very clear about our beliefs. We sought to present a rational basis for faith—not only because Protestants were questioning but especially as Enlightenment rationalism and modern science were increasingly influential in society and culture.

Catholics favored religious practices that were "not Protestant" such as Marian devotion. My Lutheran pastor friends report that in the time

3. See Crossin, "Christian Identities," 17–18, 30.

4. Williams, "Introduction," 11.

5. Williams, "Introduction," 12.

6. For more on spiritual ecumenism, see Ladous, "Spiritual Ecumenism," 1069–70; Kessler, "Ecumenical Spirituality," 91–103; Kasper, *A Handbook of Spiritual Ecumenism.*

before the Second Vatican Council, they did things that were "not Catholic." Now practices have begun to change.

The Second Vatican Council encouraged bible reading. Some Lutherans now feel free to talk about devotion to Mary. We are gradually recovering religious practices preserved by other Christians or present in earlier Christian communities.

This recovery is true of theology. At least since the latter part of the nineteenth century the Catholic emphasis was on following Thomas Aquinas. Aquinas' teaching in an attenuated form was presented in what is now called the "Neo-Thomism of the Moral Manuals." This approach was legalistic and focused on moral cases. Dominican colleagues have told me that these texts did not reflect the teaching of Thomas in its depth and beauty.

A concomitant of the renewed appreciation of the depth of Aquinas was the reemergence of other approaches to Catholic theology. The varied schools of theology have been becoming more prominent. Franciscans, for example, are taking their characteristic ways of thinking and their spirituality and relating them to today's scientific data.[7] Some of our Protestant friends may be more comfortable with a Franciscan or Salesian theology and thus we may have more springboards for dialogue.[8] The emergence of the world church and the movement toward Christian unity promise that there will be a variety of schools of theological thought reflecting diverse cultures, presuppositions, and emphases.

The rise of interest in spirituality and spiritual growth among Catholic, Protestant and Orthodox Christians has contributed to the recognition that in the days of conflict many of us might have been seeking to be a "little too clear" about our beliefs. The example of great saints teaches us that our understanding of God, of the mystery of the Trinity, is limited. The call is to have the humility to acknowledge the limits of rational models.

Younger people know these limitations. Our efforts to share our faith with them will not be effective until we present the fullness of the gospel message with humility and love. Humility calls us to admit our limitations and learn from others. Love calls us to build positive relationships and to share the fullness of the gifts that God has given us.

---

7. See, for example, Horan, *Catholicity & Emerging Personhood*; Rohr, *The Universal Christ*.

8. This volume contains numerous references to Salesian theology and spirituality.

Ecumenical Friendships

Ecumenical conversations, both formal dialogues between churches and less formal local conversations between pastoral ministers, members of congregations, and participants in ecumenical events, can lead to a variety of relationships.[9] I will offer a few considerations on these relationships. The context for many ecumenical friendships is prayer. Ecumenically minded people often pray for the guidance of the Spirit in their discussions and in their ministry together.

Ecumenical conversations sometimes lead individuals to friendship with colleagues who have the same professional or personal interests. Personal conversations often occur during the meals in formal meetings or at breaks in the common work such as helping at the local homeless shelter.

Some friendships go deeper. Common interests can lead to professors authoring books together or pastors discussing the best way to approach a parishioner suffering from trauma. Friends are a gift from God.[10]

One characteristic aspect of Salesian Spirituality is the discussion of spiritual friendship. Spiritual friendships are rare. As mentioned in chapter 2, a spiritual friend is one with whom we can discuss most aspects of life including our spiritual journey. This is not to say that they do not discuss many other matters, but that following Christ and discerning God's will are central.[11]

The spiritual director is a type of spiritual friend.[12] The progression is from direction, where one of the persons shares knowledge and wisdom the other does not yet have, toward equality where both share equally. Spiritual friends are particularly attentive to the movements of the Holy Spirit. It is the Holy Spirit who will lead the Christian churches and their representatives to a consensus on today's contested moral matters.

9. See Wadell, "Friendship," 316–18; Wadell, *Becoming Friends*.

10. See Crossin, "Ecumenical Dialogue and Relationships," 409–23, which adds depth to this brief discussion.

11. The classic text is Wright, *Bond of Perfection*. The subtitle on the cover of the 2011 printing, "The Art of Spiritual Friendship," captures the essence of the work. Stopp "Francis de Sales," 119–38, offers reflections on DeSales' friendships with Fr. Antonio Possevino, SJ (1534–1611), and the jurist Antoine Favre (1557–1624).

12. See Schemenauer, "Guide Them All," 72–93. Schemenauer summarizes: "The goals of spiritual direction for Francis de Sales are to cultivate greater love of God, which requires the evangelization of the will. These two goals provide the framework for understanding the three central themes of de Sales' direction: total surrender to the will of God, patient growth, and holy liberty" (81).

Relationality in Our World[13]

Our spiritual and pastoral relationships are taking place in a relational world. The findings of science in the twentieth and twenty-first centuries indicate that we live in a relational universe.

Albert Einstein's theory of relativity and the fact that we now speak of spacetime rather than separately of space and time points to the reality of connection. In science there is a search going on for a theory of everything. This was a quest that Einstein himself pursued—without success—in his years in the United States.

The discoveries of modern science have not been a topic of central concern to Catholic moral theologians in the past several decades except for their bearing on individual moral cases—especially in medical ethics.[14] The preoccupation of Catholic renewal has been moral methodology. My contention is that an ecumenical ethics will need to consider that humans are relational beings in a relational universe as part of the foundations for its work.

We might begin with some references to the work of Josef Pieper (1904–97), the distinguished philosopher and interpreter of Thomas Aquinas. Pieper offers an insightful interpretation of the understanding of reason and of truth. Aquinas defines the virtue of prudence as "reason perfected in the cognition of truth." In discussing this definition, Pieper explains:

> "Reason" means to him [Saint Thomas] nothing other than "regard for and openness to reality," and "acceptance of reality." And "truth" is to him nothing other than the unveiling and revelation of reality, of both natural and supernatural reality. Reason "perfected in the cognition of truth" is therefore the receptivity of the human spirit, to which the revelation of reality, both natural and supernatural reality, has given substance.[15]

Prudence is not defined as "getting my way" or "cunning" as it sometimes is these days, but as a reasonable openness to reality. The reasonable person knows reality as it is capable of being known. Some aspects of reality can be

---

13. Some of the initial material comes from Crossin, "Moral Anthropology and Human Development." For the full series of online presentations on Religion, Science, and Pastoral Ministry, see Washington Theological Consortium, "Religion and Science."

14. Schaefer, "Keeping Scientifically Informed," 175–84. Schaefer gives a concise overview of current Catholic teaching on the relationship of Christian faith and science.

15. Pieper, *The Four Cardinal Virtues*, 9.

known scientifically and others through different means—the appreciation of a work of art for example.

The wise person is open to the truth of reality wherever this may lead. The ethicist will eventually need to incorporate the truth of science into his/her thinking about morality. This should only occur after a review of the data of science as accepted in the field and critiqued by other scientists.[16] The ongoing task of ecumenical ethics will be to integrate the scientific data into the best ethical thinking. This stand may occasionally cause us to revise our ways of thinking about the human person, about her/his moral formation, or about moral issues.[17]

Josef Pieper learned from Romano Guardini "that the great German Poet [Goethe] and Aquinas both taught that reality—which is by its very nature true—is the measure of human thought and action."[18] The good human moral action is rooted then in the silent contemplation of the truth of things—including the scientific truth—that makes for wise judgment of what to do and not to do. A very important point here is that spirituality and morality should be integrated.

There is need to go deeper to address questions of human meaning. We might say, with Pieper, "that the real cannot be enclosed within any system of thought whatsoever, because it continually opens up toward something more that goes beyond it, arriving again and again at the frontier of the mysterious."[19] Thus while we can know a great deal, there are limits to our knowing.[20]

Josef Pieper preceded the current revival of VE by several decades. Yet he shares some of the same concerns. He desired to move away from the Kantian ethics of duty, from utilitarianism, and from the excessive casuistry

---

16. See Crossin, *What Are They Saying about Virtue?*, 54–58, for thoughts on the critical integration of moral theology and psychology. One should be cautious but not exclusive in integrating the findings of one discipline into another.

17. See International Theological Commission, "Theology Today," nos. 46, 80–85.

18. Schumacher, "A Cosmopolitan Hermit," 5

19. Schumacher, "A Cosmopolitan Hermit," 6.

20. This resembles in some ways the limits Thomas Kuhn sees in any scientific paradigm. See chapter 7. On the other hand, Miller, "Integral Ecology," 16–17, summarizes: "Our attitudes of love and attentiveness affect what we see and thus, what we are able to value. This is a path of transformation worth noting. Seeing can precipitate moral conversion. It is not simply a matter of our priorities following what we love; rather, it is love that enables us to see more of reality." Miller goes on to say that the positive relationship between religion and science is a recurrent theme in *Laudato si'*.

of the Catholic neo-scholastics. He wanted to offer an updated VE which focused on the good of the human person.

The practice of virtue constitutes the ultimate perfection of that capacity for the good, or better, the maximum of what a person *can* be. This anthropology presupposes an ontology of *not—yet—being* accompanied by an eschatological dimension that expresses the internal structure of human nature, which tends toward a future that is yet to come, a future in which possibilities will be realized.[21] Pieper anticipated the current revival of VE and its concern with the formation of the character of the Christian as oriented to the future as we witness in numerous contemporary works of moral theology.[22]

My contention is that an ecumenical ethics will need to consider that humans are relational beings in a relational universe as part of the foundations for its work. Our relationships with one another and with God are a primary concern. The spiritual journey of life is primarily with others even if a unique personal spiritual experience takes place occasionally. Our relationships teach us we can know the truth but our understanding is limited. Thus, we are called to humility in our journey toward an Ecumenical Ethic. We always have much to learn. Following the guidance of the Spirit lends a certain dynamism to our lives.

Science and Religion

We see that the physical world around us is dynamic and impacts our spiritual journey. We are part of an expanding universe that God is still creating.

The relationship of science and religion and its implications for moral thinking are coming more to the fore these days. The letter of Pope John Paul II to the director of the Vatican Observatory encouraged integration of science and religion and the development of a unified view of reality—but since that time the challenge to develop a unified view has not had much impact on Catholic theological statements. I presume that this observation also might be made of other Christian traditions.[23]

---

21. Schumacher, "A Cosmopolitan Hermit," 11. Schumacher mentions that Aquinas, Erich Przywara, and Martin Heidegger influenced Pieper's anthropology.

22. See Berkman and Cartwright, *The Hauerwas Reader*; Hibbs, "Josef Pieper"; Kotva, *The Christian Case*.

23. See Delio, *Birth of a Dancing Star*, 130–36.

A name still frequently mention in discussions of science and religion is Teilhard de Chardin (1881–1955). He was both a distinguished paleontologist and a Jesuit priest. Ilia Delio summarizes:

> I think the process of spiritual discernment played a significant role in his [Teilhard's] vision of faith and evolution. His "method of theology" was not too different from that of [Bernard] Lonergan: attend to experience, reflect on that experience through the intelligent mind, ponder the reflections inwardly through the structures of consciousness, and express what is contemplated by articulating new horizons of insight.
>
> Understanding Teilhard through Lonergan's "method" allowed me to recognize that without the interior component of contemplation and reflection, the dialogue between science and religion is nothing more than a set of categorical statements and ideas. Without contemplation there is no integration of experience.[24]

For Teilhard science and religion are "two ways of knowing the one world."[25] He affirms that a realistic approach to the world looks through a variety of lenses and does not limit itself to one dimension. This affirms our contention in this volume that prayer and contemplation are part of building an ecumenical moral paradigm that deals with the total reality of the universe.

Daniel P. Horan goes into detail in his considerations of a dynamic church in his chapter "The Challenge and Promise of Evolution."

> Rather than torpedo the Creator God of Christianity, the meaning of evolution offers the promise of a more catholic understanding of the human person situated within an evolving universe, connected to all other aspects of creation, and participating in an awe-inspiring history of becoming that is anything but antithetical to our faith. In fact, evolution is precisely the manner by which God desires to create.[26]

Our understanding of evolution and its implications for theology continues to develop. It goes far beyond what I learned as a young student. A view of evolution based on conflict and "survival of the fittest" is now greatly nuanced.

---

24. Delio, *Birth of a Dancing Star*, 169. For more on Teilhard, see Duffy, *Teilhard's Mysticism*; Duffy, *Teilhard's Struggle*.

25. Delio, *Birth of a Dancing Star*, 175.

26. Horan, *Catholicity & Emerging Personhood*, 63.

For example, marine biologist, Robert E. Ulanowicz, in his presentation, "Mutualism in the Darwinian Scenario," argues that "this new and wider perspective on evolution has manifold implications for science, for society, and for theology. We recognize now that we do not inhabit a clockwork universe—one in which everything is determined in a rigidly mechanical fashion by the laws of physics." And further: "One obvious advantage of a comprehensive account of evolution is that it makes room for and highlights mutuality, the precursor to love. No longer is Social Darwinism the inevitable moral consequence of evolution. The root and drive of all evolution, even of competition itself, is seen to be mutual beneficence."[27] Ulanowicz believes that the biblical tradition of God and humanity in dialogue is most appropriate to our contemporary understanding of evolution.[28]

Angela Carpenter elaborates Ulanowicz's points in her chapter 4, "Human Evolution, Cooperation, and Affect." She begins by noting that: "A group of scholars representing several disciplines including biology, anthropology and philosophy of science, are currently arguing that the modern neo-Darwinian synthesis, while still tremendously important, does not capture the complexity and diversity of evolutionary processes." Carpenter indicates that evolutionary theory is in transition from "standard evolutionary theory" (SET) to an "extended evolutionary synthesis" (EES).

She concludes the chapter saying:

> We have primarily focused on the evolution of human sociality, along with some of the distinctive aspects of human nature that are associated with sociality, such as the human lifespan, development, and plasticity. I have argued that this theoretical work is quite important for the theologian. It affirms an anthropology that attends to childhood and development across a lifespan rather than simply to adulthood. . . . And crucially, the plasticity of human development leaves open the possibility not simply for development to be shaped by general divine agency, one which naturally extends to all aspects of creation, but to a specific agency

27. The mention of "Social Darwinism" is a reference to the "survival of the fittest" now seen as an inadequate view.

28. Ulanowicz, "Mutualism in the Darwinian Scenario," 8–11. Another quite detailed, thorough, but slightly different discussion is Domning, "Chance," which is found in the same series of papers/videos as Ulanowicz. Domning offers six theological conclusions related to his presentation.

that is relational. Such openness dovetails with theological images of covenant and with God as a divine parent.[29]

Carpenter adopts the more developed relational conception of evolution of EES. This view is more open to transcendence, to a relationship with God. She says: "There is no scientific reason why the complex human affective and social system must be restricted to human relationships."[30]

She turns to the person's relationship with Christ in the Spirit. Objectively, sanctification has been fully accomplished in Christ. Subjectively, this plays out over time as the person responds to the guidance of the Holy Spirit.[31]

Theology and Relationality: The Contemporary Context

We have considered the importance of relationships in ecumenism and in pastoral care and in the scientific reality that we live in a relational universe. In this section we will move from these interpersonal, pastoral, spiritual and scientific considerations toward some further philosophical and theological reflections. These too will highlight relationality.

The context of these reflections is American individualism. Many Americans tend to look first at themselves as individuals and then as members of communities.[32] David Brooks in his best-selling book *The Second Mountain: The Quest for a Moral Life* puts it strongly in saying:

> I write it as a response to the current historical moment. For six decades the worship of the self has been the central preoccupation of our culture—molding the self, investing in the self, expressing the self. Capitalism, the meritocracy, and modern social science have normalized selfishness, they have made it seem that the only human motives that are real are the self-interested ones—the desire

29. Carpenter, *Responsive Becoming*, 94–95, 113. She has chapters discussing the relevant teaching of Reformed theologians John Calvin, John Owen, and Horace Bushnell.

30. Carpenter, *Responsive Becoming*, 154.

31. For further commentaries on the relationship of science and religion, see Haught, *Making Sense of Evolution*; Haught, *Science and Faith*; Haught, *Resting on the Future*; Barr, *Modern Physics and Ancient Faith*.

32. See Granberg-Michaelson, "Rejecting the Heresy of Individualism," 34: "The creative power of advertising in our consumer society, meshed with the tools of social media, wants us to believe that the individual is at the center of everything. . . . But here's the rub. That assumption is, in fact, foreign to Christian faith. Put simply, it's an unbiblical, alien concept."

for money, status, and power. They silently spread the message that giving, care, and love are just icing on the cake of society.[33]

The biblical tradition discussed in chapter 3 emphasizes community and relationships. Democratic freedom, once focused on political freedom, has now been identified with autonomy including the freedom to make one's own moral code. It is this extended freedom that is now being called into question by Brooks and others. Likewise, the "libertarian capitalism" which has dominated recent decades and reflects an emphasis on autonomy, lack of regulation, and quarterly dividends seems ripe for review.[34]

The question of personal and businesses's relationships to workers and to the community is now ready for reconsideration. The real world of pandemic, unemployment, racial tensions, and radical social inequality is the present context for developing further insights into human relationality.

Philosophical and Theological Reflections on Relationality

We are not able to examine the philosophies and theologies of relationality in any depth in this concise volume. The reader might look at Part I of Marcia Pally's book *Commonwealth and Covenant* for a more detailed philosophical analysis. She summarizes:

> Part I of this volume contains a short review of secular proposals that account for separability-amid-situatedness, especially by those often claimed to be advocates of one "side" or the other. On more careful reading, one finds that many were not polarizers but rather held to a mutually constitutive meld. The purpose of this review . . . is by no means to give a complete account of this secular discussion but to look at proposals for various separability/situatedness melds that have been reinterpreted through our present high separability, losing us the nuance of the original ideas.[35]

---

33. Brooks, *The Second Mountain*, xxii.

34. See Miller, "Integral Ecology," 21, where he says: "There are three major obstacles to seeing the interconnections around us. Two are explicitly discussed in *Laudato Si'*: an economic system focused on short-term profit through the production of consumer goods and a form of technology that views nature as a set of resources to be exploited. Note that Francis is not criticizing market economics or technology per se, but their narrow forms that dominate contemporary life." The third is the complex interconnections in the world around that are invisible to ordinary people.

35. Pally, *Commonwealth and Covenant*, 9.

There is a need to rebalance separability and situatedness these days as individualism/separability has become much too dominant. The epidemic of loneliness in the culture seems related to this downplaying of the importance of in-person relationships.

In the second part of her *Commonwealth and Covenant*, Marcia Pally gives an extensive review and analysis of Theologies of Relationality.[36] She offers "contemporary theologies nondenominationally as they drawn on and built upon tradition."[37] She focuses on key voices that have a relational approach. She notes that "The voices here . . . are not limited to one tradition or school but emerge from a number of starting points and standpoints. . . . Yet, their ideas about distinction-amid-relation share a family resemblance and the emphasis here is on the affinity and illumination among them."[38] The fact that this agreement is so widespread indicates that it not mere opinion but a true description of our basic human condition.[39]

She goes on to say, however, that we can always understand this condition better. No one approach can capture it. She believes, with Bernard Lonergan, that—a "plurality of interpretation—the use of science, art, humanities, and theology is needed to discern what is." This discernment has been ongoing down through Christian history. Here she calls for an "epistemological humility."[40]

In her conclusion, Pally says "In sum, the differences among accounts of relationality suggest at least three things: that differences in approach do not expunge common ground; that the common ground amid differences supports relationality as ontology; and though it may be our ontology, none has complete knowledge of it, and so we must learn from the differences.[41]

---

36. Pally, *Commonwealth and Covenant*, 123–331. She offers an extended and in-depth analysis though she does not claim to be comprehensive.

37. Pally, *Commonwealth and Covenant*, 123.

38. Pally, *Commonwealth and Covenant*, 123–24.

39. Pally, *Commonwealth and Covenant*, 124.

40. Pally, *Commonwealth and Covenant*, 124, 126.

41. Pally, *Commonwealth and Covenant*, 336. I should mention that Pally also confirms one of the contentions of this paper when she says: "Developmental psychology and evolutionary biology teach us the same curriculum: we are wired for cooperation and reciprocal giving—or, in this book's terms, relationality, separability-*amid*-situatedness, distinction-*amid*-relation. While undue situatedness, yields top-down oppression and conformity pressures, and separability yields self-absorbed greed and anomie, policies that take the two in mutual constitution proffer a life together that is more conducive to well-being than the binary alternatives" (334).

For more on the relationship of philosophy and theology to relationality, I would mention two resources.

Stephen Okey's book *A Theology of Conversation: An Introduction to David Tracy*. Okey begins by saying:

> Conversation is risky. At its best, conversation brings partners together who are committed to deepening their understanding. It might be their knowledge of the world around them, of traditions received from the past, of the person on the other side of the table or even of the self. . . . Conversation risks change that, even when it is for the better, can be frightening. . . . Such conversation is at the heart of David Tracy's theology. To start, simply reading Tracy's work is to enter into conversation with him, to participate in the back-and-forth between the reader and the text.[42]

The second recommendation is the work of John D. Dadosky. He relies both on philosophy and theological method in developing a model of "Church as Friend."[43] Dadosky combines two visions of the church [ecclesiology]: the Catholic church thinks of itself as a "communion" of people, but he argues that the church in relating to those outside should think in terms of friendship. Such friendly dialogue is a two-way communication where the participants are open to learning from one another. The Spirit is present on all sides.[44]

Work on ecumenical ethics will need to engage both unity and plurality in ethics. It will also need to engage the present and the future as well as the past. In looking to the future, Christian ethicists will need to consider how moral teaching can or might develop over time.[45]

Reflections

The preceding chapters considered the role of the Holy Spirit and the Trinity, the importance of walking with and learning from one another, and the biblical emphasis on relationships and community. This fourth chapter speaks directly of relationship: in formal and informal ecumenical

42. Okey, *Theology of Conversation*, 1.

43. Dadosky, "The Church and the Other," 302–22. Dadosky continues his exposition in subsequent articles such as Dadosky, "The Official Church and The Church of Love," 453–71.

44. Dadosky, "Towards a Fundamental Theological Interpretation," 742–63.

45. See chapter 9.

dialogues and in ecumenical friendships, in the fact that God is creating a relational universe, in philosophy and in theology, and in prayer and contemplation. I am arguing that relationality is a most important component of an ecumenical ethical paradigm.

I would note that in my conversations with others about the coronavirus pandemic several key interpersonal observations have surfaced. The pandemic has underlined the fact that Americans are dependent, for example, on communal and international relationships for food and supplies. Public discourse about the pandemic has centered on varied interpretations of freedom, of the common good, and of social responsibility.

However, pastorally speaking, people's focus has been more on protecting family members from contracting the virus and questioning whether the person him or herself spends too much time on work (sometimes with a scant salary) and not enough time on family and friendship. A related element is that working from home can provide extra time for family and friends because it eliminates, at least in metropolitan areas, lengthy commutes in traffic.

A second observation has been that while the Eucharist celebration online has been fine and safe, it is different from being with people to pray and converse. There is an undefined element missing. I wonder personally whether there is a more positive emotive element we have in the presence of others that is lacking online.

These observations in their own way speak to the importance of other people to personal well being. I would note that interaction with others is critical to one's growth in virtue both for adolescents and adults.

5

Ecumenical Foundations/Dialogues

THE WORK OF CHRISTIAN unity is the work of the Holy Spirit. The past, present, and future guidance of the Spirit grounds my optimism about the ecumenical movement. Current progress confirms this optimism. This chapter will consider recent history and then will explore several recent ecumenical documents that exemplify progress.[1]

Though the Spirit has been active since the beginning in the ecumenical movement, and the presence of the Spirit is a common experience for many Christians these days, a focus on the Holy Spirit is a recent phenomenon in the Movement.[2] As we mentioned in chapter 1, a new emphasis on the Spirit began for the members of the World Council of Churches in the 1950s. The work of the Second Vatican Council and of all such councils is rooted in the guidance of the Spirit.

Pope John XXIII's calling of the Second Vatican Council set in motion a host of processes. For example, he established the *Secretariat for Promoting Christian Unity* in 1960 under the leadership of biblical scholar Augustin Cardinal Bea. This led to the presence of Protestant and Orthodox observers and guests at the Council.

The *Decree on Ecumenism* (*Unitatis Redintegratio*, 1964) was the major ecumenical document of the Council. Also, of importance to ecumenism

---

1. This chapter draws on my article "Moving into the Ecumenical Future." I want to thank Peeters Publishers for permission to reprint parts of that text.

2. See Delaney, "From Cremona to Edinburgh."

49

were the Council's *Dogmatic Constitution on the Church* (*Lumen gentium*, 1964); the *Declaration on Religious Liberty* (*Dignitatis humanae*, 1965); and the *Dogmatic Constitution on Divine Revelation* (*Dei verbum*, 1965).[3]

Father Peter Hocken (1932–2017), a noted member of the Catholic Charismatic Renewal and expert in Pentecostalism, in his article "The Holy Spirit and the Word," reviews the twentieth century renewal in summary fashion with emphasis on the documents of the Second Vatican Council and the official documents that followed. In one prescient sentence he suggests "that we need to re-think the distinguishing features between what is essentially Catholic and what we see as essentially Protestant."[4] Our dialogue in the Spirit is already reframing how we look at one another.[5] This development of Pneumatology has continued at a brisk pace.[6]

Today's Context

In chapter 4 we considered that the American Christian churches had begun to look inward about three decades ago and mentioned some cautions Anglican archbishop Rowan Williams offered on this inward turn. For the Christian churches in the United States in general, membership and attendance have continued to decline. In the same timeframe the ecumenical dialogues themselves hit harder issues—considered unresolvable by some authors—including the divergences on certain ethical issues.

When Peter became inward-focused he began to sink. He seemed to be thinking: What am I doing out here walking on the water? When he looked outward toward Jesus he was rescued (Matt 14:22–33). Christians often blame current trends on the secularizing culture but often do not seem to be taking the time to discern the guidance of the Spirit in this present moment.

---

3. Flannery, *Vatican Council II.*

4. Hocken, "The Holy Spirit and the Word," 173.

5. See for example the most recent Agreed Statement of the Joint International Commission for Dialogue between the World Methodist Council and the Roman Catholic Church entitled *The Call to Holiness.* It has thoughtful reflections, examples of holiness, as well as citations of the *JDDJ.* It contains discussion questions for use at local and regional levels.

6. Numerous theologians are writing on the role of the Spirit. For an important analysis of the pneumatology of the noted Dominican ecumenist Yves Congar, see Groppe, *Yves Congar's Theology of the Holy Spirit.*

A paradoxical prod to self-examination is the humiliations we have suffered. The "Pedophilia Crisis" has been deeply humiliating.[7] The irony is that these humiliations can open us to the wisdom of other Christians.[8]

A further irony is that in the years of looking more inward than outward, Christian communities had an opportunity to enumerate the Spirit's gifts and to consider their communities' own deficiencies. In the ecumenical exchange of gifts encouraged by receptive ecumenism, churches can strengthen one another. This exchange can make our witness for Jesus and his message more compelling to outsiders. While it takes some institutional humility to acknowledge our weaknesses as a community, we can take great comfort in the fact that the Spirit offers us gifts through other Christian communities that can help us in our weakness.[9]

In contrast, some Christians now advocate moving into identity enclaves opposed to the modern culture. This may be the call of the Spirit to certain individuals—a call to a contemporary monasticism. This path is for the few.

Most Christians need, with the guidance of the Spirit, to help build stronger communities where they live. We need to continue to spread the gospel in the world as we find it. We are not being honest enough with ourselves about the fears which cause us to neglect the guidance of the Spirit who is moving us into the future.

The Spirit has distributed varied gifts to the Christian communities. It is in becoming one in Christ that Christians can share the gospel message most effectively and completely. As was recognized at the beginning of the ecumenical movement at the 1910 Missionary Conference in Edinburgh, a cacophony of Christian voices confuses others.

I believe that the Spirit has been at work while we have been self-preoccupied. The solutions are already present waiting to be acknowledged and implemented together—as we begin to see in the Anglican-Roman Catholic International Agreed Statement, *Walking Together on the Way*.[10] As Pope John Paul II said in his 2001 letter *Novo Millennio Ineunte*: "A spirituality of communion implies also the ability to see what is positive in

---

7. See Morneau, *Harm*, 11–19, for the effects of trauma on others beyond the immediate victims.

8. See Francis de Sales, "Humility Causes Us to Love Our Own Abjection," in Francis de Sales, *Introduction to the Devout Life*, 128–31.

9. See more below on Ecumenism.

10. See below.

others, to welcome it and prize it as a gift from God: not only a gift for the brother or sister who has received it directly, but also as a 'gift for me.'"[11]

The Joint Declaration on the Doctrine of Justification

The Spirit's guidance in the sharing of gifts is very evident in the 1999 *JDDJ*. Immediately after the Second Vatican Council official dialogues between Lutherans and Catholics began in many countries and at the international level. The International Dialogue is sponsored by the Lutheran World Federation and the Pontifical Council for Promoting Christian Unity. The *JDDJ* was the result of dialogues on justification especially in Germany and the United States followed by the International Dialogue's consideration and recommendation. The process took over thirty years and involved many leading scholars. Justification was the key theological issue at the time of the Reformation.

Susan K. Wood and Timothy J. Wengert examine the background for this startling ecumenical agreement in detail in the second chapter "The Path to the Joint Declaration on the Doctrine of Justification" in their book *A Shared Spiritual Journey: Lutherans and Catholic Traveling toward Unity*.[12]

A few pertinent points can be drawn from this chapter.

> Positively, Catholics and Lutherans both embrace the personal character of grace (a Protestant emphasis), and the creative and renewing character of God's love (a Catholic emphasis).
>
> Luther's understanding of "faith" includes what Catholics ". . . understand as faith, hope and love and term 'justification through grace.'"
>
> Thus, both the Council of Trent and the Reformers rejected security and self-conceit about one's own position and stressed the reliability of God's promise [of salvation].[13]

A crucial point is that God takes the initiative. Ecumenical convergences are the work of the Spirit and not just our own. Pope Francis believes that we should act as if everything depends on God—because it does.[14]

---

11. John Paul II, *Novo millennio ineunte*, no. 43.
12. Wood and Wengert, "The Path," 34–66.
13. Wood and Wengert, "The Path," 49, 50, 52.
14. Borghesi, *The Mind of Pope Francis*, 18.

The *JDDJ* itself, a concise and powerful document, deserves personal reading and meditation. Some key paragraphs are:

> Like the dialogues themselves, this Joint Declaration rests on the conviction that in overcoming the earlier controversial questions and doctrinal condemnations, the churches neither take the condemnations lightly nor do they disavow their own past. On the contrary. This Declaration is shaped by the conviction that in their respective histories our churches have come to new insights. Developments have taken place that not only make possible but also require the churches to examine the divisive questions and condemnations and see them in new light. (no. 7)

> Our common way of listening to the word of God in Scripture has led to such new insight. (no. 8)

> In faith we together hold the conviction that justification is the work of the triune God. The Father sent his Son into the world to save sinners. The foundation and presupposition of justification is the incarnation, death, and resurrection of Christ. Justification thus means that Christ himself is our righteousness, in which we share through the Holy Spirit in accord with the will of the Father. Together we confess: By grace alone, in faith in Christ's saving work and not because of any merit on our part, we are accepted by God and receive the Holy Spirit, who renews our hearts while equipping and calling us to good works. (no. 15)

The *JDDJ* offers a differentiated consensus. It offers a common understanding of justification in no. 15 and goes on to explicate it in nos. 19–39, saying that certain contrasting ways of looking at theological aspects related to justification are not church dividing. In doing so it offers a model that might be applied beneficially to other issues. The *JDDJ* closes by saying that there are questions that need further clarification.

Given the widespread agreement on justification evident in the affirmation of the *JDDJ* by the World Methodist Council, the Communion of Reformed Churches, and the Anglican Consultative Council, we can affirm a common basis for moving forward together:

> If Reformed, Methodist, Anglican, Lutheran, and Catholic thinkers believe their communions' statements that their different explanations of justification are compatible, although not identical, and if they believe that the communions have something to learn from each other, that shifts the possibilities for the reception of this and future ecumenical agreements. As Catherine Clifford

has argued, it becomes the basis on which the churches move forward together.[15]

The 2017 statement of the Finnish Lutheran-Catholic Dialogue entitled *Communion in Growth: Declaration on the Church, Eucharist, and Ministry* takes the model of differentiated consensus used in the *JDDJ* and applies it to other divisive issues under the headings of Church, Ministry and Eucharist.[16]

The *JDDJ* notes that change has come through a deeper reflection on Scripture. This certainly is one key part of discerning the central pillars of consensus.

Wood and Wengert suggest that:

> Catholics need to recall to themselves and to their Protestant dialogue partner that the Council of Trent clearly taught that the first grace of justification is never merited, and merit only applies to an increase in justification and sanctification, what might be better expressed today as an ever-deepening appropriation of a transformative relation to the Holy Spirit. Lutherans need to remind themselves and their Catholic partners that justification by faith alone and assurance of salvation are embedded in embodied participation in the corporate life of the church and the means of grace through Word and Sacrament.[17]

Wood and Wengert point to relationships with God and with community that are intimately related to the Joint Declaration.

Differentiation also implies tension—which can be creative as well as dissonant—but this tension need not divide a community but call it to a deeper conversion to Christ and greater love for one another including love for those who disagree with us in some matters. One example in the moral realm would be the tension between those Christians who allow room for Just War Theory in certain instances and those who hold for an absolute Christian pacifism. All Christians are called to be peacebuilders but differ on how to act *in extremis*.

---

15. Rinderknecht, "Receiving the Joint Declaration," 58.

16. See Lutheran-Catholic Dialogue Commission for Finland, *Communion in Growth*, 7–12, for background on differentiated consensus and the "Concluding Remarks," nos. 356–69, for its reflections on its differentiated consensus

17. Wood and Wengert, "The Path," 63–64.

Pope Francis' View of Tensions

In his theologizing, Pope Francis considers the polar tensions within the church. Massimo Borghesi in his book *The Mind of Pope Francis* gives a detailed analysis of the major philosophers and theologians who influenced Pope Francis and Francis's own synthesis of their work.[18]

Pope Francis's thinking allows for polarities that are in tension within the church. While some might be resolved, others continue to exist. Borghesi summarizes:

> Opposition is the lifeblood of concrete living; it brings life and dynamism to its unity. Contradiction, like that between good and evil, demands a decision, a choice: evil is not the counterpart of good, as gnosis would have it. It is its negation. The distinction between opposition (*Gegensatz*) and contradiction (*Widerspruch*) is crucial because it allows us to think of the Catholic *communio* not as a flat, uniform unity, but as a dynamic, polyform reality, which for that reason does not fear to lose its unity. Ecclesial unity is not to be understood as a monolithic block in which unity comes down from on high, in a fixed and direct manner. It is not afraid of accommodating different poles and reconciling them in the Spirit who unites everything, as in a musical symphony. This *communio* is realized in a dialogical form, in the patient development of interconnections that do not pretend to negate the accents, the variety of approaches that remain. This is the concept of the church that Bergolio found thoroughly confirmed for him in 1986 by [Romano] Guardini's philosophical anthropology.[19]

As the wounds of the Reformation are healed and the churches come together, they do so in the context of the emerging world church. The context is quite different from the time of the Reformation. There are and will be tensions as the world church emerges. Pope Francis' thinking on oppositions helps us to realize that the oppositions can be the work of the Spirit in our midst, calling us to renew our thinking and feeling.

As we move into the future together, the Christian churches could see various ways of enculturating the Christian faith. This might take place by use of differing philosophical approaches or ways of thinking. The approach

18. See Borghesi, *The Mind of Pope Francis*, 57–141, for this thought-world that differs from today's dominant Thomism. See also the polarities expressed by Francis, *Evangelium gaudium*, nos. 217–37, and the essays in Lee and Knoebel, *Discovering Pope Francis*.

19. Borghesi, *The Mind of Pope Francis*, 106.

of a differentiated consensus with its core of belief and with contrasting, op-positional but not contradictory views is compatible with varied theological schools of thought. Differentiated consensus may make for the unity in diversity of a world church.

Receptive Ecumenism

Receptive ecumenism is one of the major developments in the ecumenical movement in the last three decades. The dialogues that began after the Second Vatican Council no longer always discuss differences in their theological positions on church, sacraments, and so forth, but now might explore what the Spirit has given to one partner which can be adopted with benefit by the other.

The Fourth International Conference on Receptive Ecumenism took place in Canberra, Australia in 2017. *Leaning into the Spirit: Ecumenical Perspectives on Discernment and Decision-making in the Church* containing papers from the Conference and related works appeared in 2019.[20] It is a rich volume containing sections on the role of the Spirit, on "Contexts for Discernment and Decision Making," and on "Receiving Through Dialogue: Past and Present."

Two of the editors, Virginia Miller, and David Moxon, offer a descrip-tion of receptive ecumenism in their *Introduction*.

> Receptive Ecumenism is a method of ecumenism that focuses on learning from dialogue partners rather than being preoccupied with teaching dialogue partners. Paul Murray, the originator of Receptive Ecumenism, claims that productive ecumenical dialogue begins with introspection and an awareness of one's own deficien-cies and the possibility that one's dialogue partner can assist to correct these deficiencies. It is claimed that this process leads to ongoing shared learning and improvement. . . . Indeed, Receptive Ecumenism is commonly referred to as a movement and not mere-ly as a scholarly undertaking or an exercise in Christian praxis.[21]

They go on to characterize the conference and their book:

20. Miller et al., *Leaning into the Spirit*.

21. Virginia Miller and David Moxon, "Introduction," in Miller et al., *Leaning into the Spirit*, 1. Paul D. Murray develops the methodology of receptive ecumenism in "The Call of the Spirit," 217–34.

> The overarching theme of the conference . . . that of "leaning into the spirit" implies that it is God who will lead the Church into its fullness in grace. However, this is not to suggest that ecumenism is a passive undertaking. . . . [A]ctive ecumenism requires . . . discernment, decision making and reception.[22]

Peter Carnley, in his concluding essay to this volume entitled "Does Receptive Ecumenism Have a Future?" contends that a reasonable goal for receptive ecumenism is that "we are to be open and receptive to what may be learned from one another in such a way as to make the communion of God more fully visible. But that is surely also the goal of the twentieth century Faith and Order Ecumenism."[23] Thus the goals of these approaches elide.

Carnley quotes Cardinal Johannes Willebrands (1909–2006), former president of the PCPCU, to the effect that "The Church is the Sacrament of the of the trinitarian koinonia. She finds her origin, her model, and her goal in the triune mystery. It is from this insight of faith that we may plumb the secret of 'one and many' for the relation of local churches to each other and so to the universal church."[24]

Wood and Wengert in their discussion of the *JDDJ* point out that "The genius of the 'Common Understanding' of the Joint Declaration lies in the trinitarian framework of the agreement on justification, which situates justification within the relationships of Father, Son and Spirit and their attributed works." They go on to say that "The trinitarian framing of the consensus statement also provides the perspective and context for the resolution of remaining differences in the doctrine of justification enumerated in part 4 [of the *JDDJ*]."[25]

It is very instructive that these two major current approaches to ecumenical differences—Differentiated Consensus and Receptive Ecumenism—find their roots in the trinitarian mystery.

22. Miller and Moxon, "Introduction," 2.

23. Carnley, "Does Receptive Ecumenism Have a Future?," 249. The Faith and Order Commission is the section of the World Council of Churches that deals with doctrinal, church order, and other theological questions.

24. Carnley, "Does Receptive Ecumenism Have a Future?," 249.

25. Wood and Wengert, "The Path," 64.

Walking Together on the Way

In the context of receptive ecumenism, it is important to mention "Walking Together on the Way: Learning to Be the Church—Local, Regional, Universal" (WTW) the Agreed Statement of ARCIC III that appeared in 2017. We might quote a few conclusions from this lengthy and detailed document:

> The Commission also asks what each tradition can learn from the inheritance of the other, and how far each tradition needs to undergo conversion, renewal, and reform. This requires humility and patience. (no. 152)
>
> Each affirms a fullness of ecclesial reality at the level of the diocese gathered around its bishop, together with the relative autonomy of church at this level. . . . The trans-local organization of the churches is a clear sign that the Church wants to reach out to the human reality in the diversity of cultures, nations and even continents. (no. 153)
>
> Catholics and Anglicans must give attention to what the Spirit may be saying in the other tradition before arriving at a definitive conclusion for their own tradition. (no. 153).
>
> When, through the Church's mission in new contexts, new questions arise we need to seek out the ways in which they can best be handled. Clearly, this is important for the discernment of right ethical teaching, which takes time. This will be the focus of the next phase of the Commission's work, in accordance with its mandate (no. 160)

Ormond Rush in his Commentary on *WTW* notes, after citing the *Decree on Ecumenism* no. 17 of the Second Vatican Council, that "Receptive ecumenism invites each tradition in a dialogue to look humbly at the weaknesses and impasses in its own life, and to recognize perhaps that the other tradition lives out its life with different structures and processes that may well be gifts to be received."

Rush goes on to note seven proposals as particularly helpful for Catholics.

> The reception of the Second Vatican Council is far from complete. Many of its principles have yet to be incorporated fully into church life *ad intra* and *ad extra*. Several of the problematic areas in that reception process over the last fifty years have in fact been raised by WTW. Its proposals for a Catholic receptive learning from Anglicans may well provide help. Several of these proposals can

be selected as particularly urgent and challenging. The challenges selected here are: (1) a greater recognition of the Holy Spirit's working on all levels of the Church; (2) a greater recognition of diversity within a genuine catholicity; (3) a move towards less centralized structures of teaching and governance; (4) a greater deliberative authority afforded to regional structures such as episcopal conferences; (5) a greater participation of lay people; (6) the active promotion of genuine dialogue in the church; (7) a greater appreciation of "provisionality" and the continuing guidance of the Holy Spirit.[26]

Rush elaborates critically on each of these points raised by the text.[27] The document also lists things Anglicans can learn from Catholics.

Declaration on the Way

This critical and collaborative spirit characterizes the ecumenical dialogues sponsored by the churches. Much has been achieved. I was gratified to have had a small part in putting together the 2015 *Declaration on the Way: Church, Ministry, and Eucharist* which summarizes the work of Lutherans and Catholics in many countries.

The Declaration was a response to the call by Cardinal Koch, current president of the PCPCU, in 2011 for ecumenists to consider summarizing the work done thus far. A small group of American Lutheran and Catholic scholars compiled the DOTW over a three-year period. When it began there was no guarantee that the effort would be successful.

The American Catholic and Lutheran scholars and ecumenists found that there are thirty-two Agreed Statements, noted fifteen Remaining Differences and Reconciling Considerations, and made ten suggestions for local and regional collaboration. "DOTW is international in scope reflecting the work/prayer over the past fifty years of Germans, Scandinavians, Americans, Brazilians, and many others."[28] Given that the some of the Remaining Differences are items never formally discussed and that others seem capable of resolution, the future seems brighter than I had imagined.

One of the things I learned after the Declaration appeared was that more people than I expected had difficulties with the "On the Way" nature

---

26. Rush, "A Roman Catholic Commentary," 7, 18.

27. Rush, "A Roman Catholic Commentary," 13–19.

28. See Crossin, "Occasional Reflections," 81.

of the Declaration. The Declaration comes amid our moving towards the goal of Christian unity that we have not yet attained.

Some people have a strong need for clarity. Yet the spiritual life is a journey that is always "on the way." The most recent International Methodist-Catholic Dialogue affirms this in saying: "The journey of the Christian is a journey into the heart of the Trinity, into the perfect love which is the beginning and end of holiness." We are pilgrims on "the way."[29]

Communion in Growth: The Finnish Lutheran-Catholic Dialogue

The June 2017 Report from the Lutheran-Catholic Dialogue Commission for Finland entitled *Communion in Growth: Declaration on the Church, Eucharist, and Ministry* not only mentions the DOW but also believes "It is likely that the healing process towards a *communio ecclesiarum* will take a long time" (no. 364).

The Finnish Dialogue Commission Report mentions that "it has been able to say more than previous dialogues" (no. 367).[30] The Dialogue Commission concludes: *"It seems that a joint declaration on the Church, Eucharist and Ministry is needed as the next step, as Cardinal Kurt Koch's initiative indicates"* (no. 367, emphasis added). This is a very encouraging practical recommendation based on a detailed and compelling Agreed Statement.

The Dialogue's goal was a differentiated consensus with two distinct components:

> A clear statement on the consensus reached in the fundamental and essential content of a previously controversial doctrine.
> An explanation of the remaining doctrinal differences, which are also to be clearly named, and a declaration that they can be considered admissible and thus do not call into question the consensus on the fundamentals and essentials.

They go on to say that "It follows [from the second point] that the differing confessional positions are freed from the constraint of reaching a consensus in form and language on every imaginable doctrinal question."[31]

29. International Methodist-Catholic Dialogue, *The Call to Holiness*, no. 136.

30. See Lutheran-Catholic Dialogue Commission for Finland, *Communion in Growth*, nos. 306–69.

31. Lutheran-Catholic Dialogue Commission for Finland, *Communion in Growth*, 7–12.

One key point where the Finnish Lutheran-Catholic dialogue agreed is that baptism and Eucharist are the major sacraments. The context for this consideration is the new relationship humanity and all creation have in Christ. Christians participate in this new relationship through baptism. We see our relationship in a special way in the ecumenical convergence on the Eucharist.[32] Deeper study could bring us to a more complete understanding of the ecumenical implications of our common baptism and of sharing the Eucharist.

One question that arises is whether the method of differentiated consensus, developed in considering the doctrine of justification and now applied to questions of church, Eucharist, and ministry, can be applied in whole or in part to other divergences.

Personal Reflection—Leadership for Ecumenical Progress

The Holy Spirit has been guiding the churches over the years as we move carefully toward our goal of Christian unity. The recent documents cited above indicate to me that unity might be closer than we think.

We are on the way and needing to go deeper spiritually to cross the finish line. Francis de Sales reminds readers of his *Treatise on the Love of God* that the initiative for spiritual growth comes from God.[33] God is calling us: to go deeper in "spiritual ecumenism," and to be attentive to the guidance of the Spirit as we come closer to our goal of unity. A good context for listening for this guidance is communal prayer. The recent booklet entitled *Catholics and United Methodists Together: Shared Prayer and Resources* from the Methodist-Catholic dialogue in the United States offers a variety of prayers and services that might be helpful to all Christians. Prayerful discernment is the priority.

Lutheran and Catholic pastors have mentioned to me that even highly educated members of their congregations have little awareness of ecumenical developments since they finished their religious education. People's lives are remarkably busy and ongoing education can be limited even for the most engaged members of Christian communities. Effective ecumenical education is certainly a priority as we move toward "being one" as Jesus prayed at the Last Supper (John 17:21).

32. See Lutheran-Catholic Dialogue Commission for Finland, *Communion in Growth*, nos. 356–59.

33. See Francis de Sales, *Treatise*, 2:18.

This education will call for spiritual leadership. The Spirit works through men and women. The Spirit gifts leaders with the charism of authority. In discerning leadership for the community, we look for people to whom God has given this charism.[34]

Leaders will need sensitivity to the guidance of the Spirit, readiness to listen and learn from others, and a willingness to live with ambiguity. I believe that the Holy Spirit will give us the leaders that we need as we move toward Christian unity.

34. See Crossin, "Will Christian Unity Come Sooner?," 18–23.

6

Moral Systems

CHRISTIANS SINCE THE VERY earliest days have tried to live their moral lives in imitation of Jesus. We see in the *Didache* (c. 100 AD), for example, moral prescriptions for early Christians.[1] Of significance for our project is the fact that in the *Didache*, "Christians are not offered a choice between either right/wrong, of between being saved/damned, but between a way of life and a way of death and demands of the way of life flow from the need to love God and neighbor."[2]

As time went on, Christian thinkers such as Clement of Alexandria and Irenaeus of Lyon began to develop systematic moral thinking that would enable them to deal consistently with moral situations not addressed in the Scriptures as they knew them.[3]

Efforts at systematization in the West included the critical use of Greek philosophy. This is exemplified in the work of Augustine, of Thomas Aquinas, and of Bonaventure to name just a few major thinkers.

In his book *A History of Catholic Moral Theology in the Twentieth Century*, James F. Keenan spends an initial short chapter looking back toward the Middle Ages and noting the changes in moral thinking and approaches

---

1. See "The Didache," in Gonzalez, *A History of Early Christian Literature*, 11. He notes that this ancient concise text "reflects the practices, beliefs, and challenges of the first years in the life of the church."

2. O'Loughlin, *The Didache*, 150. His translation of the text is found on pp. 161–71.

3. The definitive listing of books of the Bible came at the Council of Nicaea in the year 325 AD.

over the time since then.[4] He says that while the long-term purpose has to do with being a Christian disciple, the nature of moral theology, however, is constantly shifting its method, its discourse partners, and its more immediate purposes.[5]

Our question in this volume is whether the Christian traditions can come together with a common moral response to Christ. Is there a common paradigm or overlapping paradigms that would enable a common response? In this chapter, we give an overview of the meaning of paradigm and discuss the dominant Catholic paradigm: natural law. We find that the many contrasting and sometimes contradictory paradigms of natural law, lead us to consideration of the paradigm(s) rooted in Scripture. The love, mercy, and peace of Jesus Christ are foundational to Christian thinking. These are preludes for a consideration in chapter 7 of Virtue Ethics as a compelling biblical ecumenical paradigm.

Moral Paradigms

In recent times, the work of Thomas Kuhn in his *Structure of Scientific Revolutions*, published initially in 1962, has had an influence not just on "hard science" but on social sciences and recently on theology as well.[6] For example, Mark S. Massa cites the concept of paradigms in using Kuhn's work to discuss the "micro-paradigm" of natural law in his 2018 *The Structure of Theological Revolutions*. In chapter 2, Massa gives a detailed discussion of Kuhn's work. Some key points that he makes include:

> Kuhn's descriptions of how science actually worked was far more historically disjunctive, and far less cumulative, than the model of the grand march of science approach had led scholars to believe....

> The basic model never claimed the loyalty of all scientists at any given moment....

> Kuhn called the exceptions to the expected and predicted outcomes of experiments anomalies—that is, challenges to the expected (and predicted) order of things defined in the dominant paradigm....

---

4. Keenan, *A History of Catholic Moral Theology*, 1–7.

5. Keenan, *A History of Catholic Moral Theology*, 5.

6. Kuhn, *Structure of Scientific Revolutions*. For a more detailed analysis of Kuhn's work, see Bird, "Thomas Kuhn."

Widespread perceptions of fundamental problems with the entire paradigm are rare, Kuhn argued. . . .

Kuhn also asserted that a paradigm ". . . is declared invalid only if an alternative candidate is available to take its place."[7]

Catholic Thinking on Natural Law

For several centuries Catholic thinking on moral issues has been dominated by the paradigm of "Natural Law." We will offer a few brief comments here.

After discussing Kuhn's work on scientific paradigms, Massa then proceeds to discuss the revolution in Catholic moral theology brought on by the promulgation of the encyclical *Humanae Vitae* on July 28, 1968, with its opposition to artificial means of contraception. The key elements of the encyclical come from the neo-scholastic interpretation of natural law.[8] Massa, taking a detailed look at the encyclical and the historical period using Kuhn's framework, believes that the micro-paradigm of neo-scholastic natural law used in the encyclical has led to a serious anomaly that has called the whole micro-paradigm into question. A revolution/crisis has begun and continues.

Massa looks at the distinctive paradigms of four significant contemporary Catholic moralists.[9] Their micro-paradigms have arisen since *Humanae vitae*. He discusses the work of Charles Curran, Germain Grisez, Jean Porter, and Lisa Sowle Cahill in separate chapters. We cannot pursue their varying perspectives here.

The voices of the natural law tradition are not limited to the four authors cited by Mark Massa. I would mention that there has been some interest in Natural Law as a foundational paradigm in Protestant circles. To cite but one example Walter Carl Still in his doctoral dissertation entitled *Natural Law Theory in Roman Catholic Theology: A Paradigm to Remedy the Crisis in the Contemporary Lutheran Ethic?* explores natural law and relates it to Luther's writings. He also contends that "The orthodoxy of theology for

7. Massa, *The Structure of Theological Revolutions*, 35, 37, 39, 41, 42.

8. For more on this school of interpretation, see Keenan, *A History of Catholic Moral Theology*, 9–34, 111–39. His discussion of *Humanae vitae* is found on 120–26.

9. Peter K. Fay, in a review article, recommends Massa's readable book that presents the revolution in American Catholic natural law thinking. In another review of Massa's book, Pablo Iturrieta of the Dominican University in Ottawa wonders whether all these models are valid representations of natural law.

Lutherans is linked to Scripture, and I believe natural law passes muster."[10] His work—now dated in certain particulars—presents an investigation pertinent to some foundational issues

A significant Catholic reflection on natural law—and the one I find most compelling—is the work of the late German theologian Eberhard Schockenhoff entitled *Natural Law & Human Dignity: Universal Ethics in an Historical World*. Reviewers are impressed with this substantive work and point to essential elements of Schockenhoff's arguments.[11]

Schockenhoff spends a large section of his work arguing for the universality of biblical ethics. He argues that biblical ethics—in particular, the Ten Commandments and the Sermon on the Mount—makes a universal claim.[12] The Ten Commandments and the Sermon offer a robust moral system that coheres well with the limited natural law theory Schockenhoff embraces.

> To speak of the natural rights of every human person is to presuppose only a modest anthropology which has nothing definitive to say about the comprehensive ends in life which allow our human existence as a whole to succeed and which helps us to realize our fullest potential. Thus, natural-law affirmations remain in a "preliminary sphere" which points beyond itself to that "fullness of the basis of life" to which the biblical revelation bears witness. This is why the natural law is the indispensable basis of an international human-rights politics, although it does not supplant the

---

10. Still, "Natural Law Theory," 12.

11. Schockenhoff, *Natural Law & Human Dignity*. Mark Graham of Villanova University summarizes that Schockenhoff's "principal objective is to defend a version of natural law capable of grounding universal moral claims while simultaneously overcoming common objections to natural law theory" (Graham, Review of *Natural Law*, 881). Schockenhoff is sympathetic to historicity but does not believe that it leads to the demise of natural law theory. Matthew Ryan McWhorter of Georgia State University points out that Schockenhoff draws from phenomenological ethicist Max Scheler contending that "the value of the human person can be demonstrated as universal, transcending yet underlying all relative historic and cultural forms in various approximations" (McWhorter, Review of *Natural Law*). This basic value leads to a limited number of *intrinsically evil actions* that violate basic human rights—for example torture, sacrifice of the innocent, rape, or adultery. The reviewers also raise a few questions. The most salient to me is Graham's question about how evolutionary theory fits together with Schockenhoff's natural law theory. See listing of reviews by Mark Graham, Mary C. Sommers, Patrick Madigan, and Matthew Ryan McWhorter in the bibliography

12. Schockenhoff, *Natural Law & Human Dignity*, 224–86.

constructions of meaning offered by the world religions and the high ethical traditions of humanity.[13]

Schockenhoff believes that the world religions and the major ethical traditions should enter dialogue and be open to learning from one another.[14]

Another important recent document reflecting this significant Catholic point of view is "The Search for Universal Ethics: A New Look at Natural Law" from the International Theological Commission of the Dicastery of the Doctrine of the Faith.[15] This accessible presentation gives a comprehensive overview of a contemporary natural law rooted in Saint Thomas Aquinas' thinking. The document concludes:

> The Catholic Church, aware of the need for human beings to seek in common the rules for living together in justice and peace, desires to share with the religions, wisdoms, and philosophies of our time the resources of the concept of natural law. We call natural law the foundation for a universal ethic which we seek to draw from the observation of and reflection on our common human nature. It is the moral law inscribed in the heart of human beings and of which humanity becomes ever more aware as it advances in history. This natural law is not at all static in its expression. It does not consist of a list of definitive and immutable precepts. It is a spring of inspiration always flowing forth for the search for an objective foundation for a universal ethic. (no. 113)

It continues by mentioning that "the concept of natural law is first of all philosophical, and as such, it allows a dialogue" (no. 114), and the final paragraph encourages

> experts and proponents of the great religious, sapiential, and philosophical traditions of humanity to undertake analogous work, beginning from their own resources, in order to reach a common recognition of universal moral norms based on a rational approach to reality. (no. 116)

This outreach by the International Theological Commission to various traditions is beyond the scope of this volume, but certainly is be encouraged.

---

13. Schockenhoff, *Natural Law & Human Dignity*, 290.

14. Schockenhoff, *Natural Law & Human Dignity*, 283–85.

15. International Theological Commission, "In Search," paragraph numbers of the document are given in parentheses.

A "common rational approach" could be of help to those seeking to build peace.[16]

James Keenan believes that at the end of the twentieth century the foundations for contemporary theological ethics in natural law thinking were well established but that understanding of natural law would continue to develop.[17] The experts who developed the International Theological Commission's Statement agree that natural law thinking needs to continue to develop in Western Christianity but also in the emerging world church.

Theological Paradigms

The use of the concept of paradigm, defined by Kuhn as "a new basis for the practice of science" is widespread as social scientists, theologians and others examine the bases of their work.[18] Three important authors whose recent writing contributes key elements to our discussion of paradigms are Michael Kinnamon, Edwin El-Mahassni, and John Meier.

Michael Kinnamon speaks of the dominant paradigm under the first General Secretary of the World Council of Churches W. A. Visser 't Hooft (1900–85) and the changed paradigm initiated by his successor Konrad Reiser (b. 1938).[19] Kinnamon suggests "In the early years of the ecumenical movement, the emphasis in the unity-justice dialectic was on the former; in recent years, the pendulum has clearly swung in the other direction. A rereading of Visser 't Hooft may help us find a better balance."[20]

Edwin El-Mahassni of Flinders University in Australia's article entitled "Kuhn's Structural Revolutions and the Development of Christian Doctrine: A Systematic Discussion," concludes:

> Thomas Kuhn's ideas on the way science progresses and develops can also be applied to understand how Christian doctrines emerge and grow. Kuhn's thoughts on normal science, puzzle solving, crisis, paradigms, anomalies, and revolutions have been applied illustratively to examples found in specific doctrines and the history of their development. . . . Furthermore, providing such a framework gives not only a more holistic approach to understanding

16. For more on peacebuilding, see chapter 8.
17. Keenan, *A History of Catholic Moral Theology*, 189.
18. Massa, *The Structure of Theological Revolutions*, 42.
19. Kinnamon, *Unity as Prophetic Witness*, 189–95.
20. Kinnamon, *Unity as Prophetic Witness*, 204.

doctrinal development, but also builds another link allowing for interdisciplinary dialogue between philosophy of science and Christian theology. Further, the work here also shows that factors external to Christianity cannot be automatically dismissed as irrelevant or inconsequential.[21]

As the conclusion of his volume, Massa has a short reflection on John Meier and Biblical Paradigms. Massa believes that Meier's magisterial five-volume series, *A Marginal Jew*, supports his own conclusions regarding paradigm change. Meier "observes that a previous generation of biblical critics simply presupposed 'neat progression' of Christological language developing in a linear way from Mark through Luke to John." Meier says:

> Once the early Christians believed that Jesus had been raised from the dead, a theological explosion was set off that assumed *both creativity and disorder for the rest of the first century A.D. When it comes to New Testament, it is best to recite this mantra: "in the beginning was the grab bag."* The next couple of centuries would be sorting out the grab bag.[22]

Massa concludes his book saying: "Thus talking about natural law is messy and chaotic, and the development of human models of it are, by definition, nonlinear because reality is always more complex than any model we can construct to explain it."[23]

The emphasis of these authors on the balance needed in the ecumenical emphasis on unity and justice, on the necessity of a holistic dialogue that is interdisciplinary, and on the fact that reality is complex and not easily captured by human models speaks to the process and the limits of constructing a paradigm for ecumenical ethics.

21. El-Mahassni, "Kuhn's Structural Revolutions," 521. El-Mahassni notes Kuhn's contextual approach to explain science. Kuhn stresses a communal dimension in scientific revolutions that is also applicable to revolutions in theological thinking in the church.

22. Massa, *The Structure of Theological Revolutions*, 181–82.

23. Massa, *The Structure of Theological Revolutions*, 184. Also see Peter C. Phan's comment, mentioned in chapter 1, on the non-linear nature of the development of thinking about the Trinity.

Personal Reflections on a Paradigm

I would say that these models of natural law present a complex picture lacking a dominant paradigm. This picture may get even more complex as we move into the world church with its varying cultures and philosophies. I believe that, just as in mathematical systems, the assumptions with which we begin affect the conclusions we draw. I sometimes wonder if natural law thinking is inextricably bound to Greek philosophy. If so, natural law might be an important micro-paradigm in some school(s) of moral thinking but not others.

I leave Massa's interesting book thinking there might be three levels of change. The first is the revolutionary change that leads to a new and distinctive paradigm. I think of Einstein's theory of relativity in science or, as John Meier mentions, Jesus's resurrection in theology. The second, also in line with Kuhn's thinking, are the regular accumulation of anomalies that lead to changes in the dominant paradigm but do not overturn it completely but modify it—such as the recent emphasis on relationships in evolution or the impact of neurobiology on discussions of moral acts. I also see room for a third level of "living with the tension" or perhaps coming to a partial consensus about the "polarities" that Pope Francis rightly sees as always present in the church.[24]

I leave Massa's book thinking that debate and discussion over natural law will be continuing. I believe that our search for a moral paradigm might best first concern itself with biblical teaching. Schockenhoff points in this direction as he discusses the Ten Commandments and the Sermon on the Mount in the last third off his book. His more circumspect view of natural law based in human dignity leads to his robust discussion of essential elements in a biblical ethics.

Prayer with and study of the biblical witness is certainly a common emphasis among Protestants, Anglicans, Orthodox and Catholics today. Contemporary Catholic foundations go back to the encyclical *Divino afflante Spiritu* of Pope Pius XII published in 1943. The 1965 document of the Second Vatican Council on Revelation commonly known as *Dei verbum* (the Word of God) develops Catholic thinking further. The bishops at the Council said that "the 'study of the sacred page' should be the very soul of

---

24. See Borghesi, "The Polarity Model."

sacred theology."[25] I would add that biblically nourished spiritual growth will be necessary as Christians work together toward consensus on ethics.

Jesus Our Savior and Exemplar

We began this book with consideration of the work of the Holy Spirit and then reflected on pastoral concerns; Spirit-guided discernment; biblical understanding; personal, philosophical, and theological reflections on relationships; ecumenical developments; and paradigms for understanding/learning

Most of the changes needed in developing an ecumenical ethics will be in the second and third categories mentioned above. That is, (2) paradigms accumulate anomalies and are then adjusted to accommodate these anomalies and (3) there are polar tensions which can lead to adjustments but not reconciliation in Christian moral thinking. The core elements common to all ecumenical moral paradigms will be drawn from Scripture. Thus, we now turn to a few considerations of Jesus as the center of our moral reflection.

Our commitment to a relationship with Jesus Christ is the key foundation for an ecumenical ethic. Jesus is the paradigmatic person.

In his writings, Saint Francis de Sales gives us much to reflect on as he discusses Jesus. Let me offer here some important insights.

Anthony Lopresti in his "Spirituality Meets Ethics: Francis de Sales and Love for God," offers an affirming yet critical analysis of DeSales' spirituality. In his "Final Evaluations," he contends:

> Francis reminds us all that a direct love of God is not only possible but positively necessary. Love of neighbor may be closely related to love of God, but it is not a legitimate substitute. According to DeSales, all Christians are called to affective love, no less than they are called to effective love. *In other words, prayer is essential to the Christian moral life.* "That which God requires of us," Francis writes to Theotimus, ". . . that among all our loves his must be the most heartfelt, dominating over our whole heart, the most affectionate, possessing our entire soul, the most general, using all our

---

25. See Flannery, *Vatican Council II*, 763–64. For a clear and helpful study of *Dei verbum* and the "State of the Questions" in the following years, see Witherup, *Scripture*. For further developments in Catholic thinking, see Witherup, "The Bible in the Life of the Church."

powers, the most lofty, filling our entire spirit, and the most firm, calling forth all our strength and vigor.[26]

For DeSales the human person is the perfection of the universe. The human person's innate love of God is the uniting faculty of the soul—as in Augustine.[27]

Francis de Sales is fascinated by the fact that we are made in God's image. Created in the image of God, men and women are loving creatures. We begin in love, act through love, and reach our completion in love.[28]

God, who is Trinity, has communicated in time. The breath of life given to us at creation by God is a breath of love.

The human person as constituted by God is other directed. We are made in the image of a triune God who is in constant communication with us. Just as God is oriented outward in loving creation and communication, so humans who are made in God's image are oriented toward others.

The main other toward whom humans are oriented is Christ. Christ is the Alpha and the Omega. All creation came into being in light of his coming. All creation will be completed in him. Jesus is the goal who gives purpose to all of creation.[29]

From the beginning all things have been created for Christ.[30] God's love is so great that he sends Jesus so that we might be united with him in glory.

Thus, we only attain to our full humanity in Christ. The gospel fulfills our deepest longings. Yet we are free and can choose otherwise. Even then God's love for us persists. Even if we sin, we can be re-created. God does not give up on us.

Francis de Sales' theology of love sees the mysteries of the Trinity, Creation, the Human Person, the Incarnation and Redemption as intrinsically linked together. All are mysteries of Love.[31]

---

26. Lopresti, "Spirituality Meets Ethics," 255, emphasis added. Lopresti is quoting Francis de Sales, *Treatise on the Love of God*, 2:156.

27. See Lux, "Augustinian Influence," 52–67.

28. Fiorelli, "Salesian Understanding," 64.

29. See Duffy, *Teilhard's Struggle*, 38–41, for some challenging reflections on Jesus as the goal of creation.

30. See chapter 2 on DeSales's Scotistic view of creation.

31. See my "Salesian Spirituality and Adult Developmental Psychology," 54–71. I should note that while Francis De Sales sees love as central, he also says in his *Treatise* that "We are created in the image and likeness of God. . . . Our soul is spiritual, indivisible, and immortal. It understands, it wills, and it wills freely. It is capable of judging, of reasoning, of knowing and of having virtues. In all this, it resembles God." Francis

We should mention here that Christian unity is very much related to loving. In his book *Costly Love* John Armstrong speaks insightfully to this point:

> Christian unity in relationships is clearly the divine design for showing the world that God loves them. When people see true love between Christians, they will believe the Father "loves" them. God loves the world and sent his Son into it as the fullest, final expression of his eternal love. Jesus did not come to condemn the world but to save it (John 3:16–17). What does Christian unity have to do with the love of Christ? *Everything*. It provides *the real-life context* in which people can "see" God's love in action.[32]

The Importance of Mercy

Pope Francis' ongoing emphasis on mercy also fits well with this emphasis on loving. In his introduction to the Jubilee year of mercy, he says:

> In the parables devoted to mercy, Jesus reveals the nature of God as that of a Father who never gives up until he has forgiven the wrong and overcome rejection with compassion and mercy. We know these parables well, three in particular: the lost sheep, the lost coin, and the father with two sons (cf. Lk 15:1–32). . . . In them we find the core of the Gospel and of our faith, because mercy is presented as a force that overcomes everything, filling the heart with love and bringing consolation through pardon. (no. 9)

He goes on to speak of the church—in my perception the church as all Christians:

> Mercy is the very foundation of the Church's life. All her pastoral activity should be caught up in the tenderness she makes present to believers; nothing in her preaching and in her witness to the world can be lacking in mercy. The Church's very credibility is seen in how she shows merciful and compassionate love. (no. 10)[33]

---

de Sales, *Treatise*, 1:91. In pastoral terms, this emphasis on Jesus' love for humanity expresses itself in devotion to the Sacred Heart of Jesus, Jesus loving all of humanity on the Cross.

32. Armstrong, *Costly Love*, 233.

33. See Francis, *Misericordiae vultus*.

Interestingly, Pope Francis and evangelical ecumenist John Armstrong arrive in the same place—they are centered in love and the mercy in action that expresses it

Our common moral paradigm(s) will focus on the virtue of love manifested in Jesus. Individual virtues such as humility, patience, gentleness, and perseverance are natural virtues that can be animated by love. It is such love that must animate the search for a common paradigm. The Spirit of Love, the Holy Spirit, the Third Person of the Trinity has given spiritual gifts for us to share with one another.

I believe that the dialogue over a common ethical paradigm will involve a sharing of these gifts. The dialogue partners will be called to a receptive ecumenism—receiving the Spirit's gifts from others and sharing our Spirit-endowed gifts with them. In this way an ecumenical paradigm will emerge.

We now turn to some considerations of Virtue Ethics as a substantive common paradigm.

7

Virtue Ethics Today

VIRTUE ETHICS OFFERS A biblically-based, philosophically, theologically, spiritually, and pastorally coherent moral paradigm that supports Christian unity and that encourages the baptized to follow the gospel daily. VE already has exponents in Catholicism, Orthodoxy, and the Protestant traditions.[1] As with any major theological school, VE has many variations/approaches around a central common core. Stanley Hauerwas showed in his early publications such as *Character and the Christian Life* that an emphasis on Christian character is consistent with certain "strains" in Protestant ethics such as the works of Calvin and Wesley.[2]

In recent decades, VE has also been enjoying a renewed emphasis among philosophers. The classical text in philosophy, one still cited decades later, is Alasdair MacIntyre's book *After Virtue*.[3]

The revival of interest in virtue is not just among philosophers and theologians. Growth in the virtues relates to the daily spiritual lives of Christians. I noted years ago that "Concern with the actor rather than just the act itself points to a crucial link of moral and spiritual theologies through the theology of virtue. Spiritual theology talks about the growth

---

1. See Crossin, "Virtue as an Ecumenical Ethic," 28–31.

2. An overview of Hauerwas's early work can be found in my *What Are They Saying about Virtue?*, 38–46.

3. MacIntyre, *After Virtue*. For a collection of other philosophers' work on virtue, see, for example, Crisp and Slote, "Introduction."

of the Christian in love for God and neighbor. It concerns itself a great deal with the positive side of the Christian life as set out by the spiritual masters . . . spiritual theology speaks very directly about growth in virtue." This growth in virtue is encouraged in friendly personal and communal relationships.[4]

VE goes back to the very origins of Christianity. Virtues are mentioned in the Bible.[5] There is a considerable history of VE.[6]

Nikki Coffey Tousley and Brad J. Kallenberg, in their article, "Virtue Ethics," note:

> In virtue ethics, the question of what kind of people ought we to be? takes priority over the question what are we to do? Virtue ethics is more concerned with truthful description of the moral life than with the theoretical construction of a normative system. A virtue approach does not reject law or rules but suggests that the application of moral rules requires the prior cultivation of good habits and skilled reflexes (namely virtues).[7]

They offer a concise history of VE and before concluding draw on Stanley Hauerwas and other authors to reflect on "Discipleship as Moral Formation through Practices." They say: "To follow Christ is not simply to imitate specific acts but also to aspire to an entire life of wisdom and moral virtue."[8]

---

4. See Crossin, *What Are They Saying about Virtue?*, 6; Spohn, *Go and Do Likewise*, 3–49.

5. Crossin, *What Are They Saying about Virtue?*, 9–11; Downs, "Vices and Virtues," 809. After referring to the contemporary renewal in virtue ethics, Downs concludes saying "the virtue and vice lists in the NT, along with the philosophical strands on which they draw, should once again spark reflection on the importance of character in the formation of Christian communities."

6. See Porter, "Virtue Ethics in the Medieval Period." Porter offers a succinct review of the sources, early Christian antecedents, and virtue thinking in late antiquity before giving a more detailed review of medieval thinkers including Bonaventure, Aquinas, and Scotus.

7. Tousley and Kallenberg, "Virtue Ethics," 814.

8. Tousley and Kallenberg, "Virtue Ethics," 818. For more on the history and the richness of Virtue Ethics see Walter, "Virtue," 1081–85. For a more detailed and focused discussion that engages both historical and contemporary sources, see Herdt, *Putting on Virtue*, 341–52. For a thoughtful and detailed exposition of a contemporary Thomistic perspective, see Porter, *The Perfection of Desire*.

Key Elements of a Virtue Ethic

In his final chapter entitled, "A Hermeneutical Proposal," of his *Biblical Ethics*, Lucas Chan discusses five common "characteristics" and four "dimensions" of Virtue Ethics. These give some indication of the breadth and depth of a virtue approach.[9] Chan goes on to link these characteristics and dimensions of Virtue Ethics to the biblical witness.

Chan also summarizes the major contributions of Anabaptist Mennonite theologian Joseph Kotva and Catholic theologian William Spohn before offering his own reflections.

What Joseph Kotva "shows, in concrete terms, [is] how Scripture and virtue ethics can be compatible and connected." Kotva deals particularly with ethics in Matthew's Gospel and in Paul's letters.[10] In an important point for our current study, Kotva notes Paul's "rather frequent employment of images of moral growth and progress, such as 'walking' and 'transforming' in Romans 6:4 and 2 Corinthians 3:18, respectively. This vision of moral growth, together with the emphasis on continuity and patterns of behavior, can become a connection point with virtue ethics."[11]

Chan offers a detailed exposition of the writings of William Spohn which is worth a careful reading. An important point for this book comes toward the end of Chan's analysis. He quotes Spohn to the point that the New Testaments speaks of the site of moral reflection as being the community and not the consciences of individuals.[12] It is usually not the individual but the faithful community together that grows in moral wisdom. This points to the need for Christian traditions to come together to discuss moral paradigms. I recommend such a discussion in chapter 9. This book is a prelude to such discussion and not a replacement for it.

Having engaged in a very thorough discussion of the elements of a hermeneutic and building on them, Chan then offers some of his own approach to the hermeneutical dimension of Virtue Ethics. He proposes his own systematic view of "how virtue ethics is relevant to reading Scripture." A few of his important ideas are as follows:

---

9. See Chan, *Biblical Ethics*, 82–92, for a detailed exposition of each of these characteristics and dimensions of Virtue Ethics. For more on exemplars, see Ellsberg, *A Living Gospel*; Williams, *Luminaries*.

10. Kotva, *The Christian Case*, 103–31.

11. Chan, *Biblical Ethics*, 100.

12. Chan, *Biblical Ethics*, 106.

Scripture shapes the reader's character as well as the character of the reader's community. . . .

The Bible is more important in forming character than in offering explicit ethical discourse. . . .

Scripture is a rich source for providing exemplary models—either explicitly or implicitly—for the cultivation of virtues and our moral formation as individuals and a faith community.[13]

Chan believes that his detailed and thorough exposition of VE as a hermeneutical tool will establish it as a bridge between the Scriptures and modern moral theology. For examples of this see Chan's discussion of the Ten Commandments in *The Ten Commandments and the Beatitudes* and the corresponding contemporary virtues he suggests.[14]

One very important point made by Lucas Chan and William Spohn is the importance of habit. I would join Spohn in noting that spiritual practices shape the character of the person.[15]

Critiques of Virtue Ethics

It is wise to pay attention to critics who point out weaknesses in a theological position or approach. In a book such as this that seeks to integrate several diverse disciplines it seems wise to take a critical but not overly critical attitude. All human efforts have weaknesses. Hopefully, critics, in pointing these out, can contribute to strengthening the joint effort.

Chan mentions some of the criticism of VE.[16] I will offer a personal affirmation of two of these criticisms. One critique is that with the burgeoning of Virtue Ethics, the reader needs to be clear about an individual author's definition of terms and conception of virtue. Philosophers, theologians,

---

13. Chan, *Biblical Ethics* 107, 109–10, 111. See also Salzman and Lawler, *Virtue and Theological Ethics*, 61–92, for a detailed discussion including a critical discussion of the work of Martin Rhonheimer. Salzman and Lawler affirm: "We grant that many of the virtues and the actions they demand and enable appear to be the same in natural and Christian ethics, but the community in which Christians learn virtues, the rainbow of exemplars for the imitation and habituation of virtuous actions, the proximate and final ends to which their virtuous actions tend, the perspective out of which they are done, all are different in natural and Christian ethics. That, we submit, creates major differences between the two" (78).

14. Chan, *The Ten Commandments*, 31–140.

15. Chan, *Biblical Ethics*, 15.

16. Chan, *Biblical Ethics*, 80–81.

and psychologists may be using common terms in different ways. I noted in my doctoral work that the psychologist Erik Erikson thinks of virtues as the different strengths needed at each of his eight stages of development during the human life cycle.[17] A theologian, on the other hand, might offer a definition of virtue based on biblical passages which rely on a person's relationship with God. These definitions overlap but they also diverge.

A second critique has to do with perfectionism. The seeker of virtues might focus on human effort and not the grace that enables a person to live the virtuous life. A person also might become focused on self—especially in a highly individualistic culture. Thus, virtue ethicists need to be clear about person's relationship with God and relationships with others in the community that are necessary for growth in virtue. Friendship is the key to spiritual growth. This includes friendship with self, friendship with others, and friendship with God.[18]

Stanley Hauerwas, in his entry on virtue in *The Westminster Dictionary of Christian Ethics*, says:

> It remains the case that we do associate certain virtues with stages and functions of life that make it difficult for any one account of the virtues and their interrelation to be satisfactory. Thus, MacIntyre argues that it is a mistake to try, as Aquinas did, to provide an exhaustive and consistent classification of virtues. Too much of our knowledge of the virtues—both as to their kind and interrelation—is empirical to make such a scheme reasonable. . . . But it is just such "untidiness" that makes many concerned with moral theory suspicious of an emphasis on the virtues.[19]

Modern moral philosophy has attempted to avoid such a subjective element in its theorizing. Virtue ethicists, Hauerwas replies, say that the emphasis of some modern moral philosophers on rules and principles has a similar subjective aspect. I would add here that a person on the spiritual journey of life does not expect clarity all the time. Life is complex and the Spirit's guidance can often seem unclear. We best look for "relative certainty" in much of our decision making rather than absolute certainty in all matters. I believe that such a stance is more realistic though sometimes unsatisfying.

Jonathan J. Sanford offers an extended philosophical analysis and critique in his *Before Virtue: Assessing Contemporary Virtue Ethics*. While it

17. See Crossin, "Salesian Spirituality," 164–70.

18. See Crossin, *Friendship*.

19. Hauerwas, "Virtue," 650.

is impossible to summarize here Sanford's clear and detailed work, we can present a few of his central ideas. He says in his "Introduction" that:

> A good case can be made that the most exciting work done in moral philosophy over the last fifty years is that set of inquiries collected under the title of "contemporary virtue ethics."[20]
>
> Its leading figures are easily recognized by . . . aspiring philosophers, with names like Elizabeth Anscombe (the movement's grandmother), Philippa Foot, Alasdair MacIntyre, Martha Nussbaum, and many others. . . . [Later, Sanford contends that the four philosophers just mentioned would now be considered "unconventional" virtue ethicists because they were opposed to modern moral philosophy while the VE movement these days embraces many of the concerns/positions of modern moral philosophy.][21]
>
> Daniel C. Russell . . . argues . . . that it is impossible to provide a definition of virtue ethics that is brief, specific, and inclusive. . . . Christine Swanton . . . specifically rejects Russell's definition of Hard Virtue Ethics as too narrow and endorses instead a view that collects all virtue ethical approaches as united by virtuous notions.[22]

Sanford, while he does not consider his work a virtue ethic, goes on to mention that he will be offering "a fresh perspective on the role of virtue within moral theorizing."[23]

Reflection on Sanford's presentation leads me to affirm somethings that was mentioned in the previous chapter. Starting points affect conclusions. A philosopher is more concerned with the clarity of reason than is a moral theologian shaped by Christian spirituality and pastoral encounters. The mystery of one's relationship with God and with human persons made in the image of God adds a subjective element that is inescapable. Christian VE will continue to have some indistinct edges! This is not to say

20. Sanford, *Before Virtue*, 1.

21. Sanford, *Before Virtue*, 1, 10–11.

22. Sanford, *Before Virtue*, 3–4. Swanton, "The Definition," 337, concludes: "The definition of virtue ethics is an important issue in the refinement of our understanding about approaches to the resolution of substantive issues in moral philosophy. Rather than closing off possibilities for creative approaches, a good definition should open space for new solutions to perennial problems. Accordingly, I believe virtue ethics should be seen as a family of moral theories with several genera and species."

23. Sanford, *Before Virtue*, 7. Sanford summarizes significant criticisms of contemporary virtue ethics, goes on to mention flaws in the assumptions about the basic tasks of moral philosophy, and then offers and overview of his project (11–20).

that Christian ethicists cannot learn a great deal from philosophers. But the frameworks are different.

Love as the Central Virtue

After reviewing some of the common criticisms of Virtue Ethics to be aware of pitfalls, we return now, building on the discussion in the previous chapter, to the central virtue of love.[24] In this I will focus on both the stages of development of Francis de Sales found primarily in his *Treatise on the Love of God* and make reference to the biblical, pastoral, ecumenical and personal approach found in John H. Armstrong's *Costly Love: The Way to True Unity for All the Followers of Jesus.*[25]

For DeSales, loving is essential to being human and "full humanness is only possible in one who loves God" (72).[26] Virtues for him are both habitual and reasonable and virtue can be further characterized as "a force and rigor that belongs to the soul as a property" (74). "Virtues found in God's friends, even though they may be only moral and natural in themselves, are ennobled and raised to the dignity of holy works by reason of the excellence of the heart producing them. In a heart that is God's friend all virtuous acts are dedicated to God" (75).[27]

In Salesian thinking, virtues most often grow gradually. The goal is a life totally dedicated to the love of God by seeking to turn everything to the good. Francis DeSales envisions a lifetime with slow, solid, and steady movement forward and with occasional setbacks as well.

"When Saint Francis de Sales speaks of love, he is generally speaking of a supernatural love which God pours into the heart. . . . This love is grace or at least grace cannot be without such love. This love is friendship with God. . . . This is not a love which can be produced naturally. . . . Such love is inseparable from the presence of the Holy Spirit though it is not the Spirit" (101).

---

24. See Sauca, acting General Secretary of the World Council of Churches, "God Is Love," 355–62, for his most helpful comments on "love that has shaped the spirituality of the Orthodox people."

25. See Crossin, "The Salesian Understanding of Virtue," in Crossin, "Salesian Spirituality," 72–122; Armstrong, *Costly Love.*

26. Page references in parentheses are to Crossin, "The Salesian Understanding of Virtue."

27. Citing Francis de Sales, *Treatise*, 2:199.

In his *Treatise on the Love of God*, Francis speaks a bit more precisely of four stages of loving. Again, the stages are not completely distinct, and one can go back and forth between them. One stage moves imperceptibly into the next.[28]

> The *first stage* is that of the neophytes: Among them are those newly delivered from their sins and firmly resolved to love God, but nevertheless are still novices and apprentices and are tender and weak. They can have affection for many distractions.
>
> The *second stage*: . . . are also souls who have progressed to some extent in the love of God and have cut away whatever love they had for dangerous things but still entertain dangerous and super-fluous loves. This is because they cherish in an excessive way and with too tender and passionate a love some things that God wishes them to love.
>
> The *third stage*: are . . . other souls who love neither things super-fluous nor with superfluity but love only what God wills and as God wills. . . . It is God whom they love, not only above all things but even in all things and they love all things in God.
>
> *Finally*, at the *fourth stage* there is the person who not only loves God above all things and in all things, but loves only God in all things, so . . . loves not many things but one thing alone which is God.[29]

Understanding and then living these stages can be difficult. They are a gift—and the higher are related to contemplation of all things in God (103–4).[30]

I should mention that when I first encountered these stages I did not understand the last two stages in any experiential way. I only understood them intellectually and I even wasn't so sure about that understanding all the time. Decades later I can see that stage 3 involves discerning God's will and then trying to do it. I am not always at this level—regularly reverting to doing it my way or the best way possible administratively. This book, whatever its strengths and weakness, is an effort to follow the inspiration—mentioned in the introduction to this book—that came to me on retreat.

28. McKenna, "Personal Religious Life," 249. He mentions that "His [DeSales] clas-sification of the stages of the spiritual life seems deliberately to lack precision, for he was capable of being most precise when this was his intention."

29. At this highest stage as we love only God in all things, we might say with Teilhard de Chardin that all things, including all the matter of the universe, are in God, and the Spirit is in them.

30. Found in Francis de Sales, *Treatise*, 2:149–52.

I should also mention that I have encountered a few people in giving spiritual direction over the years who have experienced stage 4. They have recounted to me their experience of closeness to God and are quite admirable in living the gospel.[31]

In response to the questions raised above about the relationships of virtues to one another and the possibility of focusing too much on oneself as one pursues virtues, it is important to note that Francis de Sales holds in the final redaction of his *Treatise* that there are no infused moral virtues . . . but rather that charity suffices (113).[32] I believe that DeSales' final view, following Augustine, corresponds more readily to the relationship of love and the "natural virtues" developed by human repetition that is evident in contemporary studies.[33]

DeSales also indicates that our focus should not be primarily on our virtues and our advance in virtue. Our focus must be primarily on loving God (108–9).

This final point is made for a contemporary congregation by John Armstrong, an evangelical pastor and pastoral ecumenist.

Biblical Reflections on Costly Love

In his practical and thoughtful book on *Costly Love,* evangelical ecumenist John Armstrong puts his thesis out in the very beginning: "Costly love is God's will for us."[34] Armstrong begins by noting that "relational breakdown" is characteristic of modern life. "The causes of this separation are too numerous to elaborate but I believe we are living through a culture-wide breakdown of virtue that has resulted in profound indifference. This indifference results in a lack of love of those who differ from us."[35]

Armstrong believes that our basic problems are not doctrinal differences but relational:

31. Saint Francis de Sales believed that few people reached the fourth stage of loving. Devout people experienced this stage on occasion. DeSales believed that only Mary the Mother of God experienced this fully.

32. See Mogenet, *"Un Aspect,"* 114–21, for the detailed argument comparing the two editions of the *Treatise* and DeSales' shift to a more Augustinian or Franciscan point of view on the natural virtues.

33. See the article by David Cloutier and Anthony H. Ahrens discussed in chapter 10.

34. Armstrong, *Costly Love,* xxi.

35. Armstrong, *Costly Love,* 1.

From the apostolic era to the present, it seems to me, love has *always* been the greatest struggle *inside* the church. The real struggle has not been about evangelism, heresy, money, or programs—not even discipleship, at least as it is commonly understood. *Love* has been our constant problem. Yet most everyone I know thinks our greatest struggles as Christians' concern sound doctrine, especially of Christ and salvation. Although doctrine is immensely important, it is often an excuse for a lack of love.[36]

We need to engage with our neighbors in love of Jesus and of one another. Armstrong asks: "Will our individualistic expressions of Christianity further divide the world and the church, or will we advance this 'network of mutuality' for Christian unity?'[37]

Armstrong believes that we must open ourselves to the depths of divine love, to the deep work of the Holy Spirit, and to the costs that come with this love. "We are to love as Jesus loved."[38] We are to see our doctrinal differences in the light of this love, rather than put doctrinal conclusions ahead of everything else.

Armstrong hopes that his extended consideration, his new and renewed interpretation, of the many aspects of *Costly Love* will speak to Christians everywhere. In his text, he quotes from a wide variety of Christian writers and pastors. But at the center: "God's extravagant love was ultimately poured out at a great price: Christ's total sacrifice. Such love is extravagant because it cost God everything. Such love has value beyond words."[39]

Developmental Psychology

Having discussed the central virtue of love and its development at length, we turn now to some recent work on developmental psychology. These considerations deepen our perception of spiritual growth in loving to include justice and law.

Lawrence Kohlberg (1927–87) made the psychology of moral development an important sub-field within psychology with his studies of justice

---

36. Armstrong, *Costly Love*, 97.

37. Armstrong, *Costly Love*, 3. We should note that in Francis de Sales's era, community life was presumed. He offered many reflections, however, to the original Sisters of the Visitation on their communal religious life in his Spiritual Conferences.

38. Armstrong, *Costly Love*, 5.

39. Armstrong, *Costly Love*, 10.

reasoning of young people in the United States and in other countries as well.[40] Kohlberg contended that the stages of development were universal in scope.

While we cannot delve into the manifold details in this volume, we can note that John C. Gibbs in the Fourth Edition (2019) of his *Moral Development and Reality* makes note of over one hundred research studies in over forty countries that confirm the universality that Kohlberg proposed. Gibbs affirms: "Growth beyond the superficial in moral judgment does indeed take place across diverse cultural contexts. Apparently, moral development is not entirely relative to particular cultures and socialization practices."[41]

Gibbs himself proposes four standard stages of moral development and two important adult existential areas that are not stage specific. He argues that truth and moral obligation are part of human moral development.

In his Foreword to Gibb's volume, David Moshman notes that Gibbs is a neo-Piagetian[42] as well as a neo-Kohlbergian. "He has more to say about moral development beyond the preschool years than most current developmentalists."

Moshman goes on to summarize:

> But morality, Gibbs insists, is not just about what is right and is not just a matter of knowledge and reasoning. Morality also concerns the good and owes as much to emotion as to cognition. Here Gibbs draws on [Martin] Hoffman, who highlighted the emotional side of moral development, including our deepening empathy for others. Coordinating Hoffman's theory with that of Kohlberg produces a theory that transcends both. Moral perspective-taking is recognized as simultaneously cognitive and emotional. Moral development represents progress both in justice and care.[43]

---

40. A concise discussion of Kohlberg's work can be found in Kiesling, "Moral Development," 527–28.

41. Gibbs, *Moral Development and Reality*, 82. See especially chapters 4 and 5, where he presents and analyzes Kohlberg's work in detail.

42. Gibbs offers a critical and detailed discussion of the work of Piaget in chapter 3 of *Moral Development and Reality*.

43. Moshman, "Foreword," ix. Gibbs devotes chapter 5, "'The Good' and Moral Development: Hoffman's Theory and Its Critics," to an extensive exposition and critique of Hoffman's theory. He concludes that "Kohlberg's and Hoffman's theories of the right and the good, respectively, are complementary if not integrable." Gibbs, *Moral Development and Reality*, 272.

Law's Virtues

Stages of moral development and the ongoing relevance of the previous stages which are sublated can give us some insight into moral development and its impact in adulthood.[44] Respect for law and development of virtues are concomitant at each stage of moral development with law dominant earlier in life and virtue later. Furthermore, both Kohlberg and Gibbs believe that interaction with others is essential for moral growth. Our relationships with others continue to have impact on our moral and spiritual growth throughout life.

The noted scholar Kathleen Kaveny adds to our knowledge by seriously examining the intersection of her specialties in civil law and Christian/Catholic morality. In the preface to her book *Law's Virtues: Fostering Autonomy and Solidarity in American Society* she says that her title has a dual reference:

> On the one hand, I contend that law functions as a moral teacher, as a teacher of virtue, even in pluralistic Western democracies like the United States. In such societies, I think it is particularly important that the law strive to support autonomy and solidarity, which can be understood as aspects of the virtues of prudence and justice, respectively. Autonomy and solidarity, then, are law's virtues in the sense of the virtues that human law should try to promote in our political and social context. On the other hand, I also maintain that good law must possess attributes—virtues in addition to encouraging the citizenry to act virtuously.

Kaveny quotes Isidore of Seville's (d. 636) *Etymologies* on characteristics of law. Thomas Aquinas (d. 1274) endorsed these.

> *Law shall be virtuous, just, possible in nature, according to the custom of the country, suitable to place and time, necessary, useful, clearly expressed, lest by its obscurity it led to misunderstanding, framed for no private benefit, but for the common good.*[45]

---

44. Sublation refers to the developmental process in which a previous stage of development is absorbed into and transformed by a subsequent stage of growth. Thus, elements of one stage can be preserved and reoriented in the next.

45. Kaveny, *Law's Virtues*, xi.

Kaveny says that she is trying in this text to be optimistic but not utopian and "realistic about moral disagreement without being relativistic."[46] These are goals for ecumenical ethics as well.

Kaveny stresses "the essentially social nature of human beings." The good of the community and of the individual are intertwined. She speaks of autonomy as "the commitment to be the part-author of one's life" This stance seems contrary to libertarian ideas of an all-encompassing freedom. It emphasizes the interconnectedness of people as does virtue ethics.[47]

Concluding Reflections

The underlying question raised in this section is the relationships of moral law, such as the Ten Commandments, to virtue and Virtue Ethics. Might we say that stages of early development delineated by Gibbs provide norms for action that perdure—through the process of sublation—even in the most developed human moral thinking? Thus, a comprehensive virtue ethics will need to account for the ongoing presence of moral norms.[48]

In her recent book *Ethics at the Edges of Law*, Kaveny argues that while philosophy is a privileged conversation partner of religious moralists, law might be a second such partner.[49] She says that "Taken as a whole, the book aims to demonstrate the substantive contributions that engagement with the law can make to important discussions in different facets of the field."[50]

In her conclusion she states: "[Saint] Paul's cautions and caveats about the limits of law have not eclipsed the positive aspects of law for generations of Christian theologians and pastors. Drawing on multiple roots in Jewish, Greek, and Roman sources, the Christian ethical tradition has long identified God's law with divine wisdom, and commended obedience to God's law as the surest path to human flourishing. Many important strands of Christian ethical reflection, spanning two *millenia*, have been organized around the ten commandments."[51]

---

46. Kaveny, *Law's Virtues*, 2.

47. Kaveny, *Law's Virtues*, 7, 9.

48. Some authors would make the law most important. See, for instance, the article on "Evangelical Ethics" in the *DSE* and chapter 5 in Salzman and Lawler.

49. Kaveny, *Ethics at the Edges of Law*, xi.

50. Kaveny, *Ethics at the Edges of Law*, xvii.

51. Kaveny, *Ethics at the Edges of Law*, 9.

As we see in the ancient church and in the Middle Ages, obedience to the law and the virtuous life are not opposed but complementary. I suggest that the Ten Commandments provide boundaries for moral behavior. The Commandments also indicate that certain types of activity, such as stealing the goods of others, are not virtuous. There are classic lists of immoral behaviors such as those listed by Saint Paul in his letter to the Galatians (5:19–21) and in *Gaudium et spes*, paragraph 27, that need to be considered in this regard.

In closing this chapter, we might return for a moment to the spiritual roots of morality. We might ponder the contribution of the Eastern Orthodox thinker H. Tristam Engelhardt in Kaveny's chapter, "Legalism and the Moral Life."[52]

> While rational argument has its place for Engelhardt, as do rules and principles, it is not fundamental. Instead . . . the fundamental source of knowledge is grace-filled participation in the liturgical rites and the way of life of traditional Christianity. The moral life and its rational regulations are preparatory means for the noetic experience of God.[53]

Engelhard speaks of an asceticism linked to approaching holiness. He also speaks of spiritual mothers and fathers who have significant latitude in dealing with individual moral cases of the people they guide. This resembles both Pope Francis' call for moral accompaniment of individual persons/groups and the contemporary Western revival of Spiritual Direction as important for growth.

Christian ethics as we are considering it is deeply rooted in such practices of Christian life. These are practices of doing the good both individually and as a member of the community of faith. Most change is slow. God's grace operates within us and our communities over time.

Our progress can be indistinct especially to ourselves. On an occasional retreat, we can look, perhaps with the help of a spiritual guide, at the long-term patterns evident in our lives. These will give us some indication of progress in virtue, especially in loving. We always try to remember to *pray about* and *then do* [emphasis added] the good, keeping in mind the guidance of the Spirit.

---

52. Kaveny, *Ethics at the Edges of Law*, 230–37.
53. Kaveny, *Ethics at the Edges of Law*, 232.

8

Moral Acts and the Promise
of Peacebuilding

IN THIS CHAPTER WE will discuss: the dimensions of the moral act; the importance of peacebuilding both in the world and between/within Christian churches; three virtues—inner peace, honesty, and love—that are appropriate to peacebuilding; and what peacebuilding might say to us about ecumenical ethics. We begin with a discussion of the moral act and in particular the role of reason and moral intention.

To prepare for this discussion of the moral act, we summarize some recent writing on *neuroethics* which provides part of the context for a robust contemporary discussion of moral cases. Neurobiology's data on how humans learn and how the brain works has affected the analysis of moral acts. Neuroethics reflects on moral issues in light of this neurobiological data. The study of how the brain works might cause us to rethink/nuance our traditional analysis of the moral act.

The Contribution of Neuroethics

We begin by noting that the relationship of science and ethics is discussed concisely by B. Andrew Lustig in his 2011 article "Science and Ethics." Of his many significant points, we note that Lustig, citing philosopher Ludwig Wittgenstein, says that "scientific knowledge is only one avenue for experiencing the world."[1] Here Lustig contradicts ethicists who would give an almost exclusive priority to scientific findings with little consideration of other human experiences.

Lustig continues by citing Thomas Kuhn's *The Structure of Scientific Revolutions* to note that science is not "value neutral." He concludes:

> Finally, as a matter of theological method, how does the Christian tradition best honor the integrity of its own deepest convictions when assessing issues in science and technology? Given its under-standings of God's purposes and of human nature, in a particular case, which of several strategies—prophetic resistance, thoughtful accommodation, or creative interpretation—emerges as the most appropriate expression of traditional Christian commitments?[2]

I would agree that Christians need to take a critical attitude toward the data and the claims of scientists. First, how are scientists' claims related to the data? Does the claim flow directly from the data or go beyond it? I would also ask if the study has been replicated and if so, what other scientists think about the data and its interpretation. Their in-field critique can provide helpful guidance as to how the scientific information might fit in with theological reflection.

Salzman and Lawler offer an overview of current data in their sections on Neuroscience in their book, *Virtue & Theological Ethics*.[3] They present four reasons that Christian ethicists should be interested in the "data of neuroscience." They proceed to consider the relationship of neurotheology to "attention, emotion, free will and experience."[4]

A significant point they make in the discussion of these topics is:

> The right hemisphere, it has been shown, predominantly thinks in images and metaphors, including empathy in decision mak-ing, is where metaphorical and parable experience is attended to and interpreted, and is comfortable taking risks. The left brain, in contrast, predominantly "relies on self-reflective knowing, is lan-guage-dependent and logical, removes experience from its context

1. Lustig, "Science and Ethics," 705

2. Lustig, "Science and Ethics," 708. Murphey and Brown, *Did My Neurons Make Me Do It?*, 2–3, argue that "while human reasonableness and responsibility may be explained (partially) by the cognitive neuro-sciences, they cannot be explained *away*. Rather, we should expect scientific investigation of the brain to help us understand how humans succeed in acting reasonably, freely, and responsibly."

3. Salzman and Lawler, *Virtue & Theological Ethics*, 17–28, 50–55.

4. Salzman and Lawler, *Virtue & Theological Ethics*, 18–20.

by constructing abstract, static *representations* of data, controls its environment with power derived from knowledge comprehended through practical, strategic, efficient, sequenced planning."[5]

While the authors mention that the word here is *predominant* and not *exclusive*, there is an important difference between the functioning of the parts of the brain. Moral theology today seems to be moving from highly ordered planning (left brain predominant) to more disorderly/creative personal experiences (right brain predominant).

In his 2017 book, *Theological Neuroethics: Christian Ethics Meets the Science of the Human Brain*, Neil Messer offers a detailed discussion of many relevant topics. He brings a (broadly) Reformed theological tradition into discussion of them. He argues "for a mode of engagement in which the agenda is set by theology, and scientific findings and insights are critically appropriated to contribute to a theologically shaped understanding of what it means to be human."[6]

While we cannot enter the detailed discussion of the methods of research, the data, the interpretation of data, and the varied conclusions neuroscientists reach, we will mention a few salient points that relate to our discussion of ecumenical ethics.

In chapter 2, Messer says that one of his "headline messages" is that "scientific study of the brain does not give good reasons to dismiss theological claims or reasoning."[7]

Messer notes in the following chapter that a provisional conclusion would be "this work suggests that emotion plays a large part in moral judgment, and much moral decision-making is done by automatic rather than consciously-controlled cognitive processes." Secondly, some data seems to indicate that what we experience as "reasoned moral decision making" in in fact subsequent rationalization of our intuitive judgments.[8]

In chapter 4, Messer considers issues of "free will, responsible agency and autonomy raised by psychology and neuroscience."

> To describe ourselves as sinners is to say that we radically fail to orient our lives to our truest good, and this failure has profound consequences in further failures to realize the good in our own

5. Salzman and Lawler, *Virtue & Theological Ethics* 21; the quote they cite is from Curtis, "Rebalancing the Bicameral Brain."

6. Messer, *Theological Neuroethics*, 177.

7. Messer, *Theological Neuroethics*, 11.

8. Messer, *Theological Neuroethics*, 48–49.

lives and our personal and social relationships—the privation of good in Augustinian language. As such this theological self-understanding lies at the heart of a Christian ethic: it is among other things a moral perspective.[9]

Later Messer discusses the "peculiar mix of freedom and unfreedom seen in addiction" and goes on to say, "It is God's grace that liberates our bound wills."[10]

I would speak of the work of the Holy Spirit in this regard. While Messer stresses Augustine on sin, I would tend—most likely because of my "Salesian Optimism"—to give more emphasis to grace. I agree with Messer in his conclusion that the different schools of theological thought—he cites virtue ethics and natural law theory—could have fruitful discussions of how best to engage neuroscience.[11]

In this section we have noted that cognitive neuroscience cannot "explain away" human reasonableness and responsibility; that emotion is very much intertwined with cognition; that science can give us a deeper understanding of the brain but does not "dismiss" our theological reasoning and conclusions; that some of our moral decision-making is "intuitive"; and that addiction can "co-opt and subvert our willing, choosing and acting." This background prepares us to discuss the classic dimensions of the moral act.

The Moral Act

We gave an extensive consideration to Virtue Ethics in the previous chapter. We concluded that the positive approach of VE offers a helpful paradigm for an ecumenical ethics. We concluded further that, given the empirical data of the psychology of moral development and the practical interaction of good civil laws and virtue, we should consider the importance of moral law and incorporate it into our virtue paradigm as part of human moral development.

We now will present the classical model of the moral act which is often used to consider both virtuous and sinful actions.

The model—drawing on the Scriptures and dating back to the Middle Ages—speaks of the object, the circumstances, and the intention of the act.[12]

9. Messer, *Theological Neuroethics*, 99.

10. Messer, *Theological Neuroethics*, 102–3.

11. Messer, *Theological Neuroethics*, 180.

12. Crossin, "Moral Actions," 71–74, 78.

the *object* of the act, that is the objective of the act, and the moral goodness or evil as measured against biblical criteria or other traditional criteria;

the *circumstances* (including consequences) of the act; and

the *intention* of the person performing the act.[13]

The object and circumstances of the moral act were considered in detail in Catholic moral theological debates in the decades after the Second Vatican Council.[14] More recently, attention has focused on reason itself.

In her excellent article, "Moral Reasoning in 'the World,'" Christina G. McRorie summarizes the literature and offers an approach toward handling the difficulties. She notes that "Even if these critiques of reason are not intended to be devastating, however, they nonetheless have raised substantial concerns about whether and how we ought to 'trust' our rational capacities, given their malleability and corruptibility."[15] She goes on say "Catholic moral theology is . . . reevaluating its long-standing confidence in human reason, most recently in light of a growing awareness of the deleterious effects of social sin."[16] She cites Daniel Day's observation that social structures and relations influence "not only the agents' habits, but also their very 'deliberations,' and eventually their conscience itself."[17]

McRorie proposes that an "Epistemic Humility" which opens itself to grace can help to mitigate these concerns. This would involve "listening to the voices and experiences of precisely those who have been affected by distorted rationality at work in theology." These may be the poor or others who have been excluded. "Specifically, in receptively listening to their experience, we may be exposed to insights we cannot see within our closed contexts, and therefore gain new perspective on the perniciously conditioned and imperfect nature of our own reasoning—even if this new perspective is uncomfortable."[18] I believe that such listening will need to become part of the process of ecumenical dialogue on ethics lest the dialogue partners stay captive to unconscious cultural/moral presuppositions.

---

13. See *Catechism of the Catholic Church*, "The Morality of Human Acts," nos. 1749–56.

14. See Salzman, *What Are They Saying about Catholic Ethical Method?*, 26–47.

15. McRorie, "Moral Reasoning," 215.

16. McRorie, "Moral Reasoning," 216–17.

17. McRorie, "Moral Reasoning," 223.

18. McRorie, "Moral Reasoning," 235.

Another concern that has been raised about moral acts refers to their "circumstances." Jean Porter in her essay on "The Moral Act in Veritatis Splendor," mentions that "it is not at all clear how we are to distinguish object from circumstances in the description of a particular action." She goes on to say "The determination of the object of the act presupposes that we have described the act correctly from a moral point of view, and that process requires normative judgment about the significance of different aspects of the actions. In other words, the determination of the object of an act, is the *outcome* of a process of moral evaluation, not its presupposition."[19]

Another focus is on the person's "intention" in acting and the factors that make the person responsible for her/his actions. This focus is consonant with the call to walk with people and get to know them individually.

Persons engaged in ministering to others can begin to have a sense of the moral/spiritual development of the person or persons with whom they are walking. Many factors influence spiritual development and moral responsibility such as family upbringing; genetic predispositions to illness; the impact of traumatic events; the development of our brains—which lasts into our twenties; the impact of conscious and unconscious feelings; and so forth.

All the factors just mentioned—influences on reasoning, the act and its circumstances, factors influencing intention—deserve critical and deep study. Any ecumenical group working on moral discernment will need to take a careful look at these factors and act with "Epistemic Humility."

We also should mention three other aspects of individual moral decision-making. First, while some moral decisions are clearly for good or ill, others are not-so-clear. For difficult decisions, the discernment discussed in chapter 2 is necessary.[20]

Secondly, "Relational models of systematic moral analysis, grounded in Scripture-tradition, and including the findings of modern science, could provide a different framework within which to consider the object, circumstances and intention of moral acts."[21] The possibility of change in moral analysis based on the relational context points to the fact that Christian ethics has developed over the centuries and will continue to do so.[22]

---

19. Porter, "The Moral Act," 225, 227.

20. See Crossin, "What Does God Want Us to Do?," 145–49.

21. Crossin, "Moral Actions," 74.

22. See chapter 9 for reflections on development of doctrine.

Thirdly, it is well to recall that there is a necessary balance between the rights of the individuals and their responsibility to the common good.

> The creation story declares that every person is made in the image and likeness of God. Inherent in the dignity that God bestows on each person are both rights and responsibilities. We have a right to life itself and rights to basic human needs that make life livable, such as food, housing, healthcare, education, and safety. The flip side of rights are responsibilities. Each person has certain responsibilities toward other persons, society and the common good. Catholic social teaching contends that to be human is to experience not only certain rights but also obligations toward people and the community.[23]

We see the need for such balance today in the discussions of pandemic vaccines, of libertarian capitalism, of the environment, and of other moral issues.

Baptized into a Community

Going even deeper into our communal relationships and responsibilities, we can note: our relationships as Christians include our being part of Christian communities. We are baptized into a community of belief. Interestingly, Christians, despite our differences, tend to recognize one another's baptisms. At a basic spiritual level, we are joined to one another.

Pope Francis had some salient comments on community at his January 30, 2021 meeting with Italian catechetical officials. He devoted the third section of his remarks to community.

> It is only by rediscovering a sense of community that each person will be able to find his or her dignity to the full. Catechesis and proclamation cannot but place this community dimension at the centre. This is not the time for elitist strategies. . . . This is the time to be the artisans of open communities that know how to value the talents of each person.

> What I referred to then as Christian humanism also applies to catechesis: it "radically affirms the dignity of every person as a Child of God, it establishes among all human beings a fundamental fraternity, teaches one to understand work, to inhabit creation as a

---

23. Morneau, *Harm*, 26.

common home, to furnish reasons for optimism and humor, even in the middle of a life many times more difficult."[24]

Communities can be places where persons are valued and personal gifts can flourish, or they can be places where prejudices and negative actions decrease freedom and limit human possibilities. Humans flourish in peaceful contexts. Good moral judgments come from peaceful hearts and honest relationships based in love of God and neighbor. Thus, we move forward now to consider inner peace, peacebuilding in society, the importance of honesty, and our foundations in loving.

Peace of Heart

Given our extended consideration of personal moral acts and our membership in both spiritual and societal communities, we now will explore the virtue of inner peace and its external manifestation in peacebuilding.[25]

One important aspect of Jesus' message of love, mercy and humility is that it is of contemporary relevance in 'building peace.' The presence and proclamation of the gospel of Jesus Christ includes inner peace and peacebuilding.

In the Gospels the risen Jesus says to the disciples: "Peace be with You." The story in John's Gospel of the original gathering of disciples reflects the experience of all disciples: the proclamation of the message of peace does not necessarily dispel disciples' fear. (John 20:19–29) The disciples need proof that this is the Jesus they knew. "Thus, closely associating a gesture with His greeting of peace, Jesus shows them his hands and his side. The message of Mary Magdalen has been confirmed by their own experience." Thus, the disciples came to inner peace. Jesus gives the Holy Spirit to be with the disciples in the world and guide them.[26]

Disciples are to be the bearers of the fruits of Jesus victory to the world beyond the characters and time of the story of Jesus. The reader is aware that the Spirit is in the community and will remain with the community forever, but the community must reach beyond its own borders to continue

---

24. Francis, "Address, January 30, 2021," quoting his Address at the Fifth National Conference of the Italian Church, Florence, November 10, 2015.

25. For more on specific moral issues, see Lee and Dearborn, *Discerning Ethics*. This text is described in chapter 9.

26. Moloney, *The Gospel of John*, 530–31.

the mission of Jesus.[27] The community of the baptized living in imitation of Jesus and following the guidance of the Holy Spirit flows outward in acts of charity that include building peace in the neighborhood or in the world.[28]

This peace is primarily a gift of the Holy Spirit that we should ask for but also is a fruit of our daily spiritual focus and our efforts to give everything over to God. Peacefulness often flows out of a life of prayer where we take as much time listening to what God might be saying to us as we take offering petitions for those in need.[29]

For Francis de Sales this emphasis on inner peacefulness flows out into gentleness with others. Thomas Donlan notes that "as Francis's various objections to Catholic militancy coalesced in the early 1600s, the concept of *douceur* (gentleness) emerged as the core principle of his vision for a nonviolent, Christ-centered Catholicism." While opposed to Protestantism, DeSales viewed it as a pastoral challenge and not a military one. "Although attracted to Catholic militancy in his youth, Francis had slowly but surely become a prophetic advocate for a non-violent Catholicism in an era of Militancy." The Visitation sisters founded by Francis de Sales and Jane de Chantal in 1610 were/are a community dedicated to living and sharing this gentleness.[30]

A "Gentle Peace" can be both in our hearts and in our midst.

Peacebuilding

In recent decades Christians have been giving greater importance to ongoing communal efforts at peacebuilding between the Christian churches and in society at large. The ecumenical movement over the last century has been a successful international effort in building peace rather than continuing religious strife and divisions. Jesus' teaching and actions point toward a much greater emphasis on building peace nonviolently rather than sustaining conflict.

The biblical foundations for peacebuilding are numerous and compelling. Ron Sider in his lucid and concise book *Speak Your Peace: What the Bible Says about Loving Our Enemies* offers an extensive biblical argument

27. Moloney, *The Gospel of John*, 531–36.

28. See Chan, *The Ten Commandments*, 209–17.

29. See Francis de Sales, *Introduction*, Part III. For references to peace, see Francis de Sales and Jane de Chantal, *Letters of Spiritual Direction*, 187.

30. Donlon, "Order of the Visitation of Holy Mary," 35, 45.

that Christians are called to be peacebuilders. He says: "Does Jesus ever want his followers to kill? Should Christians ever use violence to resist evil and promote peace and justice? When Jesus commanded his disciples to love their enemies, did he mean that they should never kill them? These are the central questions of this book."[31]

Pertinent insights from his book include:

> The chapter provides abundant evidence that the earliest church, as reflected in the New Testament, did not forget or neglect Jesus' message of peace. Christ brings peace to the worst ethnic hostility of the first century, that between Jews and Gentiles. There are echoes of the Sermon on the Mount in several different places. Again and again, the New Testament calls Christians to imitate Christ—precisely at the cross. And in faithfulness to Jesus' teaching that his disciples must love their enemies to be children of our heavenly Father, Paul states clearly that at the cross, God loves his enemies.

> Only the liberating power of the Holy Spirit can transform self-centered sinners into persons capable of truly loving their enemies. Biblical pacifism is grounded in supernatural grace, not natural human goodness.

> Nonviolent action works. A recently scholarly volume by Erica Chenoweth and Maria J. Stephan explored all the known cases—323 of them—of major armed and unarmed insurrections from 1900 to 2006. Their conclusion? "Nonviolent resistance campaigns were nearly twice as likely to achieve full or partial success as their violent counterparts."[32]

Interestingly Sider argues that both "just war" and "pacifist" Christians, despite their differences, should work together on "nonviolent just peacemaking" for the common good.[33]

We should note that one of the latest documents of the Joint Working Group of the WCC and the PCPCU is entitled "Peace is a Treasure for All."[34] We should also note the theme of the WCC for the last seven years has been "The Pilgrimage of Justice and Peace."[35]

31. Sider, *Speak Your Peace*, 13.

32. Sider, *Speak Your Peace*, 70, 132, 126.

33. Sider, *Speak Your Peace*, 150. See Cook, "War," for an interesting presentation of three different views on these related topics.

34. This 2022 study document is found on the websites of the WCC and the Dicastery for Promoting Christian Unity [formerly PCPCU].

35. See the website of the World Council of Churches.

Peacebuilding is an ongoing process not only a necessity in crisis. Our goal would be to build relationships that prevent differences from coming to violence. An example of this is the Interfaith Council of Metropolitan Washington, DC. The Council came into being when at a crisis moment where life was in danger, local Christian and Jewish leaders realized that they had no contacts with leaders in the Muslim community who could help diffuse a very dangerous situation. This incident led subsequently to Catholic, Protestant Christian, Jewish, and Muslim leaders coming together in 1978 to form the Interfaith Council [IFC]. The IFC now brings together eleven historic faith communities to promote dialogue, understanding and community and to work on projects of common interest throughout the DC region.

My own experience in eight years of service as a Catholic representative on IFC's Board was most positive. I learned a great deal about the member religious communities. I attended monthly meetings that rotated to the churches, synagogues, mosques, and temples of the members. I always attended the luncheon before the meetings to get to know some of the Board members personally, and to sample the communities' food! These encounters were defining moments for me that later led, for example, to conversations with the Hindu community while I was serving at the Catholic Bishops Conference.

Spiritual Dimensions of Peacebuilding

Peacebuilding for Christians has deeply spiritual foundations. Theologian and Pastor Howard Thurman (1899–1981) teaches about the spiritual dimension of nonviolence. Myles Werntz's article, "Prayerful Resistance: Howard Thurman's Contemplative Nonviolence," explores the spiritual foundation for Christian living and acting.[36] Thurman's "interfaith community" in San Francisco was devoted to "personal empowerment and social transformation through an ever-deepening relationship with the Spirit of God in All Life." In meeting Gandhi, Thurman was most impressed with the mystical roots of Gandhi's thought that enabled the activism that confronted injustice.

"A nonviolent approach to racism and violence is possible, Thurman believed, only because of a transformative encounter with God. . . . In the mystical encounter of prayer, not only do people transcend the doctrinal particularities which divide Christians . . . in prayer people are driven to

36. Werntz, "Prayerful Resistance," 26–29

confront the core issue of violence—the self-righteous and egoistic self. The ego is thereby displaced from its throne, replaced by the desire for union with the beauty of God. Our false selves are un-done and we realize the dignity of every person."[37] The slow work of contemplation puts Thurman in the company of people like Thomas Merton, Henri Nouwen and Dorothee Solle.

Laurie Cassidy augments Thurman's understanding in her "Contemplative Prayer and the Impasse of White Supremacy." She argues for an expansion of our consciousness which will make us more self-aware. This growth in knowledge of the conscious and unconscious defenses of white supremacy is concomitant with a growth in the knowledge of God. She draws on the Carmelite Spirituality of John of the Cross in noting that "the contemplative journey of dark night is a deeply engaged process of passionate desire and critical exploration which makes possible new patterns of relationships not only with God but also with one another."[38]

My own observations, in the practice of spiritual direction, is that moving closer to God's love/mercy in meditation and contemplation—or more precisely, letting God move closer to us—is a long-term endeavor empowered by the Spirit.[39] The discernment of the Spirit is evident in action which leads to deeper prayer and then to further action. Deep spiritual roots enable the ongoing pursuit that peacebuilding requires. The alternative can be a short-term attitude of "been there, done that" or coming to "burnout" from the deep, often stressful commitment necessary for peacebuilding.

The Importance of Honesty

A virtue related to humility, honesty with ourselves and others, is not much valued in public discourse in the United States these days but is absolutely essential for peacebuilding. "Scripture upholds honesty as a quality closely related to excellence of character. The habitual practice of honesty is necessary for harmonious relationships. The Scriptures associate honesty not only with truth-telling but also with the pursuit of justice and faithfulness in interpersonal interactions."[40] Both familial and societal relationships

37. Werntz, "Prayerful Resistance," 27.

38. Cassidy, "Contemplative Prayer," 115, 118, 123.

39. For interesting reflections on Salesian mysticism and Scripture, see Dailey, "A Song of Prayer," 65–82.

40. Cochran, "Honesty," 374. Also see McCarthy, "Truthfulness," 795. McCarthy

depend on truthfulness for their stability. While there are rare exceptional cases where a person might speak falsehood, the binding nature of honesty is the overwhelming consensus of both Old and New Testaments.

Philip Kenneson goes a bit deeper when he writes of Christian worship enabling us to speak more truthfully.

> It is by means of the formation that takes place most fundamentally in worship that the *ekklesia* learns to recognize and name its idolatry as idolatry. Whereas much contemporary life is devoted to exalting and extending the reign of the gods of fashion, convenience, efficiency, novelty, violence, excess, fear, and insecurity, the *ekklesia* is called to devote itself to worshiping the only true and living God.[41]

In worship the congregants can encounter the basics of truthful speech. Our speech takes on the quality of its surroundings whether they be social media or the gospel.

Father Lucas Chan, SJ, in his *The Ten Commandments and the Beatitudes* discusses Exodus 20:16," "You shall not bear false witness against your neighbor." Chan notes that the there are two parallels to this commandment in Deuteronomy (17:2–7; 19:15–21).[42]

Chan mentions that Patrick Miller in his book "points out . . . the first text [Exodus] in that it reflects the primary context in which the commandment operates—the administration of justice. It also spells out the worse possible consequences of uttering false and harmful words—namely, killing of the innocent."[43] The book of Deuteronomy in the two texts just mentioned fleshes out the commandment to protecting poor people. Honesty in speech can serve as a protection for members of the community. "Our work shows that its core moral value lies in the protection of the reputation and dignity of our neighbors through our spoken (and unspoken) words."[44] Christians are called to examine their speaking from personal and/or cultural presuppositions that may be prejudiced.

A retired ambassador who spoke in my class years ago shared an experience of not-total honesty. He had been called back to serve on a team

---

mentions that both the letters to the Colossians and to the Ephesians urge Christians not to lie. We are to speak the truth in love.

41. Kenneson, "Gathering," 63.
42. Chan, *The Ten Commandments*, 113.
43. Chan, *The Ten Commandments*, 113.
44. Chan, *The Ten Commandments*, 117.

of mediators of conflict in a distant part of the world. After much effort, his team was able to get many of the principal players in the conflict into conversation with one another. When each spoke, he talked about the fact that his people were the victims of the others. No groups were perpetrators, all were victims. How could it not be so as they had been taught about their victimization in school when they were young. Sadly, the former ambassador reported that this teaching of distorted history was still taking place with the mutual anger, hatred, recriminations, and conflicts that recurred among the groups with regularity.

Dishonest history can have deleterious effects for coming generations. On the other hand, public processes of engaging the truth, difficult as they may be, can help short-circuit generations of dishonesty as we see in the various Truth and Reconciliation efforts throughout the world.

Love Our Neighbor and Our Enemy

As we mentioned earlier, the law (the commandment) provides a boundary. It alerts us that we may be heading off course. At times we need such warnings. But what we are seeking more deeply is love of neighbor and even of enemies without recriminations.

The model for our speaking is Jesus and how he spoke to and treated others. We might note that his was a healing presence and hope that our speaking the truth will be for the healing of ruptures in the community.[45]

Jonathan Wilson-Hargrove in the final chapter of his *Reconstructing the Gospel: Finding Freedom from Slaveholder Religion* speaks of nonviolent love and not letting our opponent become our enemy. The *confession, resistance, and nonviolent love* that he advocates are not easy. It is not easy to separate "slaveholder religion" from the "Christianity of Christ."[46] We see here the agenda for our spiritual journey. We need to let go of our past habits and attitudes to embrace new ways of thinking and living based on the virtues of peace, humility, honesty, and love.

Interestingly, the theme of the WCC's Eleventh Assembly in 2022 is "Christ's love moves the world to reconciliation and unity." It is, says Susan Durber, "the first such theme to put love at the heart of the assembly."[47] She 'believes that putting this "language of the heart" at the center of our

45. Chan, *The Ten Commandments*, 119–20.
46. Wilson-Hartgrove, *Reconstructing the Gospel*, 155–70.
47. Durber, "Christ's Love Moves the Church," 365.

ecumenical efforts might resonate deeply in the world church—especially beyond the bounds of "Western" ways of thinking. A focus on Christ's love could bring us all together.

Such love can animate us. It also encourages us to prepare rather than "to jump right in." Pastor Ginger Gaines-Cirelli in her book *Sacred Resistance: A Practical Guide to Christian Witness and Dissent* reflects on the spiritual roots and practical implementation of "Sacred Resistance."

Pastoral Preparations

Gaines-Cirelli speaks to both the individual and communal dimensions of this process in a clear and thoughtful way. This process is or needs to be "driven by love and relationship."[48] I would recommend her "Chapter 4: Prophetic Guidance for the Living of These Days" with its clear exposition of the in-depth preparation needed for taking a "prophetic stance."

Gaines-Cirelli's "Chapter 6: What Do We Do" considers both the process of discernment and practical courses of action by/in a local congregation or community. In summary:

> As with the decisions related to when and what to speak, choosing when and how to actively engage in the public square requires intentional discernment. I've emphasized: study, engaged communal life, staying informed, guarding against confirmation bias, and prayer as tools for discernment. If we are discerning whether to take a personal action, whether to attend a rally or march, to sign a petition or open letter for example, these tools will be very important and helpful to self-monitor your motives, your integrity, your tolerance for risk, your level of commitment and your hope.[49]

The ongoing process of peacebuilding calls for a variety of virtues such as hope, patience, courage, humility, and inner peace to name just a few and the kind of preparation and collaboration mentioned by Jonathan Wilson-Hargrove, Ginger Gaines-Cirelli, and others.

---

48. Gaines-Cirelli, *Sacred Resistance*, 15.
49. Gaines-Cirelli, *Sacred Resistance*, 96.

Personal Reflections: Embodying Virtues

Peacebuilding calls for an ongoing life of prayer, for the practice of virtues, and for practical preparation. It also calls for personal discernment. We can, with the assistance of a spiritual director or a spiritual friend(s), discern whether we are being called to peacebuilding and if so, what gifts God has given us that would be helpful in peacebuilding. We noted in chapter 2 that we can't give what we don't have. It is important to spend some time noting our gifts and how they might best be utilized in the local situation of conflict or potential conflict.

The discernment relates to the bigger question: "What is God calling me to do?" If we have inner peace and joy in our times of prayer and discernment, we have one of the classic signs that the Holy Spirit is guiding us. This gives us some, but not absolute, confidence in our discernment.

We seek to be part of the solution of problems rather than being part of a "chorus of complaint." Christian churches today have a series of internal problems. Respect for the moral teaching of the churches is not strong. Our discernment could relate to how we can improve this situation. Can we work with others to build peace within Christian communions and across denominational lines? Part of my purpose in writing is to encourage dialogue, collaboration, and ecumenical ethical paradigm-building that, with the guidance of the Spirit, can bring Christians together.

One sign of progress in this regard might be a cultural return to honesty. I think that I learned to be honest by osmosis as much as by instructions from my parents. The osmosis might have come from my grandfather and father in seeing and hearing how they conducted business. The customer was to be treated fairly and honestly. Money was to be given to the church collection and to charity. Sins were to be acknowledged and confessed. Virtues such as generosity, honesty, and love were to prevail.

I once read a short article in a religious publication that noted that with the decline in church membership or attendance, people were hearing less and less about fairness, honesty, generosity, charity, peace of heart and other virtues. It used to be said that "Repetition is the mother of learning." It takes repetition to understand and then to embody virtues. We need to see them as I did as a boy, hear about them, and then try to put them into practice. This practice calls for a vibrant spiritual life in a community whose good example shows that all are seeking to follow Christ in loving and supporting one another.

9

Ecumenical Reflections on
Moral Discernment

THIS CHAPTER WILL DEVELOP our reflections on moral discernment in the churches. These reflections will include two of the documents of the Faith and Order Commission of the World Council of Churches that appeared in recent months.[1] These are volume 1: *Churches and Moral Discernment: Learning from Traditions*, and volume 2: *Churches and Moral Discernment: Learning from History*.[2] We will also refer to three other important recent works and say a few words about them. I will offer my moral reflections throughout this chapter and continue them in chapter 10. I will conclude with a proposal that some of the churches that have endorsed the *JDDJ* establish a Working Group to develop an *Ecumenical Ethical Paradigm*.

In 2015 in an article for the *Journal of Ecumenical Studies*, I reviewed many then-current reflections on moral discernment.[3] This overview will not be repeated here. But I will offer further considerations based on the 2013 F&O document *Moral Discernment in the Churches: A Study Document* before looking at volumes 1 and 2.[4] There are numerous items in these three texts that will be helpful to our current discussions.

1. I wish to thank the World Council of Churches Publications for their permission to quote extensively from volume 1 and volume 3 in their recent series of documents.

2. See the bibliography for more detail on these documents.

3. Crossin, "Ecumenical Reflections," 561–82.

4. Faith and Order Paper 215 is also found as an appendix to volume 1 in the new series from the F&O mentioned above.

Moral Discernment in the Churches offers some "Background" on the WCC's "Way toward a Study of Moral Discernment" which complements our earlier reflections.[5] The text also offers an important "Clarification of Terminology."[6] It mentions and discusses—in line with the text's objective to discuss the discernment process—numerous practical moral cases which are presented throughout the text separately in boxes as thirteen "examples."

The *Moral Discernment in the Churches* text begins by offering four reasons, which we must keep in mind, why moral consensus is so difficult to attain:

1. Moral questions reflect deeply held theological beliefs about sin and human nature.

2. Moral questions are often encountered within the context of personal experience and are therefore likely to be deeply emotionally charged.

3. Certainty about the rightness and wrongness of one's own or another's position on a moral issue—whether based on the authority of church teachings, spiritual guidance, or individual discernment—can make dialogue across lines of difference extremely difficult.

4. Churches engage in the process of moral discernment in culturally and ecclesiologically distinct ways that are often not known or understood by one another.

In its text focused on practical experience and on the obstacles to dialogue, *Moral Discernment in the Churches* affirms that "There is a general recognition of the existence of universal truths."[7]

The text also affirms four statements drawn from the WCC study, *Christian Perspectives on Theological Anthropology*. These are in line with our discussion of relationality in chapter 4. They add a final point—not drawn from the Anthropology document—which says, in part: morality, as the discerning and acting for the good and the right, is the way in which human persons navigate through both the meaning-affirming and the meaning-threatening relationships in which they find themselves.[8]

5. F&O, *Moral Discernment in the Churches*, nos. 1–8.

6. F&O, *Moral Discernment in the Churches*, nos. 12, 13.

7. Both the four points and the mention of universal truths are found in the *Introduction* to moral discernment in the churches. Our previous discussions of natural law, of the Ten Commandments, and of moral development point in the direction of some universal truths.

8. F&O, *Moral Discernment in the Churches*, no. 24.

The text then moves on to discuss well-known sources for moral discernment both those that come from "Faith Sources" and those derived from "Human Reason and Other Sapiential Sources." It follows the section on Sources with discussion of some "Causative Factors in the Disagreements." "The first category [of Causative Factors] includes social and ecclesial factors that shape and affect communication. The second category includes factors stemming from different approaches to moral discernment."[9] It is here in the text that the examples appear and are pertinent to the discussion. They provide real cases and not just abstractions.

Reflections

In reflecting on these two sections of Causative Factors, we learn that it is important for dialogue partners to get to know one another personally. Sessions might include (1) sharing of one's personal experience of the question being discussed or (2) her/his feelings about the issue under discussion or (3) any stereotypes that he/she knows they bring to such discussion. I believe that if a moral consensus is ever to be achieved, underlying personal and communal issues need acknowledgement and processing.

In attending dialogues over the years, I noted that there was often time for informal discussion. This occurred over meals and sometimes in evening sessions that were more social in nature where a variety of church-related questions could come up. These sessions were more personal and experiential. In such an atmosphere, personal concerns could come to the surface.

Such questions need to be prayed over as well as discussed with colleagues informally. The Spirit can speak in unexpected ways. Ecumenical colleagues who forged agreements on justification and other important issues had to resolve issues like the ones presented in *Moral Discernment in the Churches*. The fact is that, not without considerable effort on the part of the dialogue partners and with the guidance of the Spirit, we have come to agreements on many matters and can do so on moral issues as well.

The *Conclusion* of *Moral Discernment in the Churches* points to the reality that there is common ground as well as obstacles.[10] There are common sources in Scripture, tradition, and the "hard" and "soft" sciences. This common ground can lead to common commitments, to "light brought into darkness" for the well-being of others.

9. F&O, *Moral Discernment in the Churches*, nos. 75–85.

10. F&O, *Moral Discernment in the Churches*, nos. 87–110.

Some suggestions in the document include the "greatest recommendation" that "structured dialogues about the process of moral discernment" should take place. The authors also suggest that dialogues "seek to reflect on the same issues from the other's perspective." Awareness of church cultures and their impact on dialogue is also recommended as well as recognition of the fact that people make moral arguments in diverse ways.

My own suggestion is structured dialogue. I believe that a task force with expertise in various moral sources and drawing expert members from the world church, might explore issues raised in this report and the others that follow it. A task force might also address issues raised by the Orthodox mentioned in my 2015 article. A smaller group(s) is more appropriate in the beginning of what might be an extended process.

Churches and Moral Discernment.
Vol. 1: Learning from Traditions

This 2021 document presents essays on how moral decisions are made in fourteen Christian traditions—authored by their own experts. It is meant to be informative and "enable conversation and mutual listening" and "giving an account of the sources of authority and ecclesial structures involved in moral discernment." It is well to note that "the self-descriptions . . . do not provide an exhaustive account of the various traditions nor of their moral discernment processes."[11]

Rachel Muers and Kristina Mantasvili in their "Introduction" to this volume make helpful observations of the fourteen papers as a whole:

> All the papers here recognize the Holy Spirit, scripture and tradition as core common sources for moral discernment that are intrinsically connected, forming the heart of moral discernment in the churches. It is striking that the work of the Holy Spirit is . . . often not referred to explicitly when churches give detailed accounts of how these processes work. (xviii)

> All of the papers indicate the use of at least some kind of "tradition" (small t) as source for moral discernment. (xix)

> The moral norms, at various levels, that are appealed to, revised, or developed in a moral discernment process are all carried by tradition—sometimes confessionally specific and sometimes shared with other churches. (xix)

11. F&O, *Learning from Traditions*, ix–xiii.

> It is striking how many of the papers in this volume, in describing a
> church's approaches to moral discernment, make detailed reference
> to its history and the contexts in which it has been found. (xx)[12]

Given these helpful insights into the whole document, we will focus
further comments on those Christian traditions that have formally endorsed the *JDDJ*. This gives them a common "platform" on which to build.[13]
Our emphasis will be primarily on issues relating to moral thinking and not
on ecclesiology.

We might begin with the essay on Jeremy Worthen on "Anglican
Moral Discernment" as it indicates some important topics (identified in
bold). Excerpts from other essays pertaining to the topic follow.

Scripture, Tradition, and Reason[14]

- Worthen notes that "Anglicans have often identified scripture, tradition, and reason as the three primary sources for moral authority. . . . The unique authority of Scripture is clearly indicated. . . . He
  goes on note that "such 'tradition' was valued primarily for its ability
  to enhance the understanding of scripture and to furnish customs
  for the church in areas where scripture did not prescribe or indeed
  was silent." Christians need to be prepared "*to discern* in the complex variety of their circumstances the choices that will keep them
  faithful to Christ."[15]

- Morag Logan in her treatment of "The Role of Theology in Moral
  discernment" in Methodism, says "Wesley also recognized the significance of human experience, especially Christian religious experience
  in theological discernment." These four—scripture, tradition, reason,

---

12. Rachel Muers and Kristina Mantasvili, "Introduction," in F&O, *Learning from Traditions*; page numbers are in parentheses.

13. The essays are Jeremy Worthen, "Anglican Moral Discernment"; Josef Romelt, "Catholic Ethical Teaching: Between Infallibility and the Sense of the Faithful"; Bernd Oberdorfer, "Respecting the World, Engaging in the World: Basic Principles of Lutheran Ethics"; Morag Logan, "The Role of Authority in Moral Discernment" (Methodist); Rebecca Todd Peters, "Sharing Power to Discern the Will of God in Every Time and Place" (Reformed).

14. I wish to thank World Council of Churches Publications for permission to quote extensively from volumes 1 of their series of documents on moral discernment.

15. Worthen, "Anglican Moral Discernment," 82.

experience—are now referred to as the "Methodist Quadrilateral." Scripture is preeminent.

- Rebecca Todd Peters notes that "a Reformed theological perspective holds that human understandings and interpretations of the gospel do change and grow as the human community changes and grows."[16]

- Joseph Romelt, in his "Catholic Ethical Teaching," remarks "human beings hold to the unchangeable word of God. And yet we still need to unlock its sense anew considering the challenges of our own time. Therefore, the insights into the fields of moral theology and its form in actual practice are ever changing."[17] He concludes his essay by saying: "the sense of faith of all the members of the Catholic Church is proving to be the actual framework for triggering a deepening insight into ethical consequences of faith."[18]

I note here a coherence in recognizing the fundamental sources of moral theology with Scripture being at the center. I would mention that, in line with our common emphasis on spiritual ecumenism, our understanding of the inspired Scriptures can always go deeper.

Synodality

- Worthen mentions that Authority has been a major topic in Anglican-Catholic dialogue. He goes on to speak of "Synodality" and its development in the Anglican tradition since the nineteenth century. The role of the laity in these synods has increased over the years since then.[19]

- Josef Romelt in his essay explains the meaning of magisterium in the Catholic Church at some length and what it does and does not mean. It is important to note that there has never been "a solemn dogmatic declaration on an ethical topic."[20] While the focus is on the Pope and bishops there is a significant role for the laity as well. The Catholic church under Pope Francis has encouraged Synodality and has encouraged surveys of laity before recent synods.

16. Peters, "Sharing Power," 76.
17. Romelt, "Catholic Ethical Teaching," 45.
18. Romelt, "Catholic Ethical Teaching," 48.
19. Worthen, "Anglican Moral Discernment," 85–86.
20. Romelt, "Catholic Ethical Teaching," 40.

- Marag Logan's essay speaks of the deeply conversational style of Methodism. "In Wesley's understanding, one cannot be a Christian alone." Methodists have a "strong social understanding" which manifests itself in the complex structure of connectionalism, which in turn expresses itself in local, regional and national conferences. Conferences "have the authoritative voice and decision-making power for the church."[21]

- In her essay on Presbyterianism, Rebecca Todd Peters shares that "representative councils (sessions, presbyteries, synods, assemblies) . . . govern the life of the community." Presbyterians affirm that discernment takes place in community.[22]

Each of the communities, and the Lutherans also as I have personally experienced, value the thinking of the members of the community. Forms of Synodality should encourage moral discernment that listens for the voice of the Spirit speaking through the members of the community.

The Role of Bishops and Clergy

- Worthen also mentions *the importance of the clergy and especially bishops.* He refers to the "distinctive ministry of bishops 'in relation to doctrine, worship, and moral life.'"[23]

- For Methodists, however, the role of bishops eroded over time. While now Methodist bishops do sit in council, they have no authoritative voice though they can address the members of the church through position papers or pastoral letters.[24] We should note that Methodist bishops in the United States do have the power to assign clergy—which is not the case with other Protestant denominations.

- In Presbyterianism, the "indwelling of the Spirit" suggest the basic equality of clergy and laity. *Teaching Elders*—Ministers of word and sacrament—and *Ruling Elders* have equal status and work together. The general assembly holds authority that "seeks to protect our church from errors in faith and practice."[25]

21. Logan, "The Role of Authority," 121, 123, 124.
22. Peters, "Sharing Power," 72.
23. Worthen, "Anglican Moral Discernment," 86.
24. Logan, "The Role of Authority," 125.
25. Peters, "Sharing Power," 75.

- The Catholic Church is well known for its Magisterium of the Pope and the bishops. Romelt explains what this does and does not mean in some detail.

- Berndt Oberdorfer would emphasize the limited nature of the church's "competence to prescribe moral norms." This does not mean that the Lutheran churches do not stand for moral norms but that their implementation falls to the conscientious individual.[26]

Binding Force of Church Teaching

- Worthen mentions that ARCIC II states that for Anglicans "the greatest possible liberty of informed judgment, and that therefore official moral teaching should as far as possible be commendatory rather than prescriptive or binding."[27]

- Along these lines, Berndt Oberdorfer mentions that the Lutheran Augsburg Confession in article 28 states that the bishop should be preaching to convince not coerce.[28]

- These stances contrast with Catholics who offer arguments that they hope are persuasive in authoritative documents but also expect that church teaching will be followed.

- Rebecca Todd Peters summarizes the Presbyterian view in saying: "Because members of the Presbyterian tradition believe that the Holy Spirit works through elected leaders to help illuminate the truth of the gospel for our times, the authority represented in these councils and their statement is voluntarily accepted as the wisdom of the church."[29]

Informed Moral Judgment

- In Worthen's essay there is emphasis on *"informed" moral judgment.*[30]

26. Oberdorfer, "Respecting the World," 67–69.
27. Worthen, "Anglican Moral Discernment," 86–87.
28. Oberdorfer, "Respecting the World," 62.
29. Peters, "Sharing Power," 78–79.
30. Worthen, "Anglican Moral Discernment," 87.

- Oberdorfer mentions also that the memorandums from the *Evangelische Kirche in Deutschland* which are not normative . . . aim toward the formation of conscience. Conscience ultimately guides church members.

I would note here that regarding the topics of bishops and clergy, authority, and informed moral judgment, a both/and approach can be helpful. Yes bishops, elders, and clergy have a charism given by the Spirit for leadership. And this leadership cannot be exercised apart from the community and the movement of the Spirit in the community. The leader listens for the guidance of the Spirit.

The conscientious Christian must act as appropriate to the situation. Oberdorfer's conscientious decision making seems to parallel Aquinas prudential decision making as does Bonhoeffer's penultimate discussed below. All stress the importance of individual situations. Of course, the wise decision maker draws on common church teaching and theological expertise in making important moral judgments. We apply Jesus' teaching in some difficult situations, such as disconnecting a ventilator from a family member, where determining absolutely the "most loving thing to do" can be cloudy. We pray and do our best.

Penultimate

Oberdorfer cites Dietrich Bonhoeffer and his use of the category of "penultimate" to characterize questions of worldly decision making. Oberdorfer summarizes Bonhoeffer when he says: "The sphere of 'works' very seldom requires an exclusive 'either/or.'" Mostly it is a sphere of "more or less," that means it implies a spectrum of possibilities that are "more or less" appropriate expressions of Christian love. We cannot decide in advance what is more and what is less. It depends on context, which might also change. This idea is fundamental to Paul's ethic: "everything is lawful but not everything builds up," and "test everything, hold fast to what is good."[31]

Peters reflects some similar concerns from a Presbyterian point of view when she says of the wisdom of the church that:

> While all such statements and positions are the result of a considerable process of discernment, they remain provisional reflections

---

31. Oberdorfer, "Respecting the World," 65. This seems parallel to Aquinas' reflections on relying on the virtue of prudence for individual cases.

of our best human judgment and discernment at the time and stand open to further illumination and reform in light of the on-going life and experience of the people of God and the work of the triune God in the midst of human life.[32]

Bonhoeffer and Peters both refer to what we have called "relative certainty."

A Common Moral Theology

The five Christian communities whose scholars' essays we excerpted above seem to have convergence on much more than justification. *All in practice have the inspired Scripture at the center and emphasis on tradition, reason, and experience as they judge appropriate.* Of course, the ways that these sources interrelate are varied and worthy of further discussion.

I would summarize here what I have said earlier in this work:

- The literal sense of Scripture should be taken seriously but using the historical critical method as well as narrative approaches to the text help us to get to the meaning of the text. These approaches should be used critically. As Scripture study evolves, we should adopt methods that give us a deeper appreciation of God's word. We need to interpret the Old Testament in the light of the New Testament.[33]

- Tradition and Scripture are linked, and the traditions of the churches manifest—often directly but sometimes obliquely—the gospel message.

- Reason has played an important part in Christian morality since the ancient church began to systematize Christian thinking. Current developments in our understanding of the close link of reason and affect needs to be explored and their impact on Christian ethics considered.[34]

While the Catholic Church seems to be sorting out how synods will work in practice, synods and their cognates are standard for the signatories of the *JDDJ*.[35] These communal meetings involve a host of representative voices. One challenge to the decisions of these gatherings appeared in the

32. Peters, "Sharing Power," 79.

33. See Davis, "Biblical View of Covenants," 631–48.

34. See the essay by Cloutier and Ahrens cited in chapter 10 for their development of this connection.

35. See section on synodality in chapter 10.

recent Catholic synod on the Amazon. According to some public reports, Pope Francis did not affirm one of the suggestions of the synod because he believed that it originated not so much from the discernment of the guidance of the Spirit as for administrative reasons [my terminology].[36] As a long-time administrator myself, I can affirm this administrative tendency of wanting to get things over and done clearly in a short period of time. I agree with Pope Francis that we must "listen for the guidance of the Spirit" and not let other considerations take over the process.

I would like to mention that there is need for further *articulation of common criteria for personal and communal discernment of God's will.* Years ago, I encountered some colleagues who were attending their national denominational meeting. They were coordinating how they would communicate with each other by cell phone during the meeting. Their conversation reminded me of Democratic and Republican political conventions. I wondered if church politics would be part of their conversations. If so, I wonder how these conversations would relate to discerning God's will. And I also wonder about the influence of secular cultures. In developing a paradigm for moral decision making in a world church, how will we account for the influence of cultures and their benign and questionable influences?

The role of bishops and other clergy in approving church teaching is standard in some Christian communities. For others, clergy participate in the assembly as voting members along with lay participants and the Assembly has authority to approve church teaching. Lay participation is most important as those who have the charism of leadership/authority seek God's will for the community.[37] While authoritative structure may vary, as they do for instance in Catholic religious communities and in Protestant local communities, certain key elements such as listening to the members of the community and discerning the guidance of the Spirit are *sine qua nons*.[38]

---

36. This example could point to a problem with having only clergy as voting members of synods. Clergy tend to be administrators as part of their ministry. Lay experts should have a vote in the synod and share in its discernment and consensus.

37. See Harmon, "Baptist Moral Discernment," 111, cited in this volume. "Authority for Baptist ecclesial moral discernment is primarily located in the local Baptist congregation. . . . [L]ocal Baptist churches can and should take into consideration the efforts at ecclesial moral discernment undertaken by other local Baptist churches, . . . Baptist unions, as well as . . . other Christian communities."

38. See section on synodality in chapter 10.

The further question that arises is around the charism of authority.[39] If individuals or a group has been called by the Spirit, has the charism of authority, and has listened to the community in discerning the guidance of the Spirit, should not the default position of members of the community be to follow their teaching rather than to disregard it. I would think that their teaching should be presumed correct and that, while conscientious dissent is possible, it should be highly informed by consultation, study, prayer, and discernment like that of those who have received the charism.

Pope John Paul II's call to other Christians in his 1995 encyclical *Ut unum sint* sought a patient dialogue on the forms his ministry could take that would "accomplish a service of love for all concerned."[40] The question for all of us is: how shall those with the charism of authority work together and exercise their spiritual authority for the moral good of all Christians and their surrounding communities? Here we should note that Christian moral decision-making has an impact on members of the community who are not Christians, and that impact must be taken into consideration out of love for our neighbor.

After these reflections, we move to consider volume 2.

Churches and Moral Discernment.
Vol. 2, Learning from History

The second text, also released in 2021, considers changes in moral teaching over the centuries. Nineteen scholars were asked to provide essays. These essays deal with usury (3), slavery (3), church-state-society (4), war and nonviolence (3), women in liturgy (1), marriage (3) and suicide (2).

In their preface, Myriam Wijlens and Vladimir Somali note that differences on moral questions can become a "threat to an existing unity or prevent the restoration of Christian unity."[41] These divisions can impede unity. They also can be an impediment to spreading the gospel message.

---

39. I should note that Cecil M. Robeck Jr., in his essay on Pentecostalism entitled "Word, Spirit, and Discernment," says that the Assemblies of God' Constitution for the General Council suggests that "the interpretation and application of the biblical text lies first in the hands of those who are recognized as members of this "divinely called and scripturally ordained ministry" (140).

40. John Paul II, *Ut unum sint*, no. 95

41. Wijlens and Shmaliy, "Preface," ix.

The hope is that by analyzing concrete examples a deeper understanding of "similarities and differences in moral discernment processes" can develop. The scholars were to consider how processes of moral discernment were involved during the controversy as well as in its resolution. They were to answer questions such as: What triggered a tradition to engage in a process of reconsidering a moral position? How did the process evolve? Who was involved in the decision making? What helped the tradition to avoid division as the change occurred over a certain period?

Simone Senn, in her "Introduction," summarizes the nineteen studies and what has been learned. For example, the Faith and Order study group learned that many traditions might have held one position on a specific topic at one time and shared a common but different position years later. But the argumentation leading to the new position might differ greatly. Studies on usury in this volume exhibit this phenomenon.[42]

Senn concludes with "Insights Emerging from the Study Process." These include the fact that a new perception/understanding of the phenomenon led to a change in moral teaching. For example, the understanding of economics shifted and so did the teaching on usury. Likewise, psychological insight into suicide led to changed pastoral practice.

A second reason for change is the churches' moral failures. Examples here include the churches relations to slavery or to the state in the Nazi era. "The churches realized that they undermined their calling to witness to the gospel by being complicit in a system of power and hegemony, and thus contributed to moral failure."[43]

A third reason for change has been the realization that the church is not upholding the dignity of the human person. This grounds the Roman Catholic Church's embrace of religious freedom at the Second Vatican Council in the "Decree on Religious Liberty."

A related aspect of the third reason is a deeper appreciation of the call of service to vulnerable people. "The change in the Mennonite tradition from passive nonresistance to active nonviolence is a case in point."[44] Senn goes on to speak of Orthodox attention to *oikonomia* (a certain pastoral flexibility and benevolence in applying norms) and *akriveia* (precise application of norms) in applying moral norms. "Pastoral discernment focuses on the question of what will contribute to healing and salvation of the

---

42. Senn, "Introduction," xv.

43. Senn, "Introduction," xxiii.

44. Senn, "Introduction," xxiii–xxiv.

person . . . as for example in the case of a Christian soldier."[45] In Malaysia, the question was how the Methodist church was to move from focusing on itself to focusing on being welcoming to others.

The authors of this text, which is rich in historical detail and ecumenical understanding, hope it will help the churches as they engage with today's moral questions.

Further Ecumenical Resources

The three Faith and Order documents discussed above provide a wealth of ecumenical resources for deeper dialogue on moral issues. They will be most helpful in working with divisions that already exist. I should mention that the goal of this volume is to begin to develop a forward-looking moral paradigm that representatives of Christian churches can use as a framework for evaluating new moral issues or revisiting old ones. This is not to say that the foundational elements of a paradigm will not be of help in discussion of current moral differences.

There are several other recent resources that could be mentioned. I will note three of them.

The appearance of the new 2021 *Oxford Handbook on Ecumenical Studies*, edited by the late Geoffrey Wainwright and Paul McPartlan, brought with it a fine essay by Michael Root of the history of the discussion of "Morals." Root offers a concise overview of the work on "Social Ethics in Conciliar Ecumenism," including the international meetings of the Life and Work movement and the ongoing and developing efforts of the WCC.[46]

He moves on to consider the significant work done in bilateral dialogues in ethics and follows with the three particular dialogues whose statements are most comprehensive.[47] These are the "The Ecumenical Dialogue on Moral Issues: Potential Sources of Common Witness and Divisions" of the Joint Working Group between the Roman Catholic Church and the World Council of Churches";[48] the most comprehensive result of dialogue which is the ARCIC statement "Life in Christ: Morals, Communion and the Church";[49] and the most comprehensive national dialogue from the

45. Senn, "Introduction," xxiv.

46. Root, "Morals," 326–32. I refer readers to this quite helpful historical background.

47. Root, "Morals," 332–36.

48. Published in 1998.

49. Published in 1994.

Catholic-Protestant Mixed Commission in France entitled *Ethical Choices and Ecclesial Communion.*[50]

Root notes that the Joint Working Group and ARCIC statements "argue that churches need to share general ethical principles or have shared values and a common vision. What they do not need to share are the more specific norms and judgments that are based on those principles or values."

He also mentions that the French statement indicated that specific differences such as those on sexual ethics and authority of ethical teaching "have lost much of their power to separate."[51]

Root himself contends that both general principles and specific norms—including those on some difficult issues—would need to be part of an ecumenical ethics. I agree with this observation. I also note that the three key articles Root cites along with the recent statements of both the Anglican-Catholic International and American dialogues provide necessary background reading for those developing an ecumenical ethical paradigm.

Considering Divisive Issues

The recent book *Discerning Ethics: Diverse Christian Responses to Divisive Moral Issues* edited by Hak Joon Lee and Tim Dearborn adds significantly to our discussion in chapters 8 and 9. Most of the text is devoted to sixteen controversial issues in social ethics each of which is discussed at some length.

The essays all follow the same format. Each author—different authors discuss each question—presents the issue and then three or four varied responses to the issue. The author seeks to give a fair presentation of each point of view. The authors, each with some relationship to the *Fuller Theological Seminary* in California, conclude with their own response to the issue in question. The authors bring a breadth of knowledge to these controversial topics.

The Introduction by editor Hak Joon Lee sets the stage for the work and is worth serious reflection. "Even while we believe in one God, serve one Lord, pray in the one Spirit, and read one book, we are often radically divergent in our understanding of God's will on particular social issues." He goes on to say that preachers "do not want to upset people, but the outcome

---

50. Published in 1992
51. Root, "Morals," 336.

is that many Christians are more influenced by secular ideologies . . . than they are by the corporate spiritual formation by their congregation."[52]

Hak Joon Lee says that Christian need to be "self-reflection and self-critical" of their own positions on issues.[53] He goes on: "In summary, one may say that ethical reasoning is a kind of art or skill necessary for discipleship. . . . Every ethical decision should be pursued prayerfully and communally in the love of God and others, and be open to mutual testing, correction, affirmation, and challenge from brothers and sisters in Christ. . . . Our goal is to help readers to better understand other Christians through the study of a wide spectrum of today's urgent social issues with global awareness, open-mindedness, and respect. For this, we think dialogue is the best approach."[54]

Later Lee remarks that "Ethical reasoning" is "neither always clear nor necessarily black and white." He goes on to say: "In Christian ethics, ethical reasoning and variable selection is closely associated with ethical method, which involves the theological and philosophical basis of ethical reasoning."[55]

In his afterword, co-editor Tim Dearborn makes the crucial point: "In worshiping Christ as Lord, Christians subordinated the authority and influence of Caesar. Likewise, in our ethical positions, we are called to make sure that we are not bowing our knee to any political party, social ideology, national loyalty, or personal self-interest."[56]

This volume complements the work of the documents and volumes cited above and provides insight into the dialogues ahead. It is well to keep Dearborn's cautions in mind as we move forward in developing an ecumenical ethics.

We turn now to development of doctrine, an important question raised by the F&O's volume 2.

Development of Doctrine

Jesuit Historian John W. O'Malley, after writing major volumes on the Councils of Trent (1545–63), Vatican I (1869–70) and Vatican II (1962–65), compares them in his insightful reflection: *When Bishops Meet: An*

52. Lee, "Introduction," 2.
53. Lee, "Introduction," 5.
54. Lee, "Introduction," 6.
55. Lee, "Introduction," 8, 10.
56. Dearborn, "Afterword," 320.

Essay Comparing Trent, Vatican I and Vatican II. Of particular interest for our work is his reflection on the development of doctrine. His scholarly work provides additional understanding that moral teaching can and does change over time.

O'Malley mentions that the long-standing attitude in the Catholic Church was that the church teaching does not change.[57] This stance began to falter:

> When in 1943 Pope Pius XII published his encyclical *Divino Af-flante Spiritu*, he validated historical and archeological methods for the study of the Bible, which was an implicit validation of similar approaches for other areas of sacred studies. Bit by bit, scholars began to show that every aspect of church life and teaching had been affected by change.[58]

O'Malley goes on to note that by the beginning of the Second Vatican Council theologians and bishops took change for granted. "Their only questions were about how to explain it, about how far it could legitimately go, and what the criteria were for making changes."[59] O'Malley continues by mentioning the forms of change.

> This keener sense of historical change took three forms in the [Second Vatican] council, captured in three words current at the time— *aggiornamento* (Italian for updating or modernizing), *development* (an unfolding or evolution, sometimes the equivalent of progress), and *ressourcement* (French for a return to the sources}. A basis assumption [was that] . . . [t]he Catholic tradition was richer, broader, and more malleable than often perceived in the past.[60]

Dei verbum, the Council Document on Divine Revelation, mentions "progress" and "growth" specifically in no. 8. "Tradition is not inert but dynamic."[61]

A singular resource for this change was the *Essay on Development of Doctrine* by John Henry Newman (1801–90). As we have seen, the Second

---

57. O'Malley, *When Bishops Meet*, 46–47.
58. O'Malley, *When Bishops Meet*, 48.
59. O'Malley, *When Bishops Meet*, 49.
60. O'Malley, *When Bishops Meet*, 50
61. O'Malley, *When Bishops Meet*, 52.

Vatican Council endorsed Newman's "central theological idea, the development of doctrine."[62]

As biographer Eamon Duffy mentions, Newman was the first great
theologian

> not merely to grasp the importance of the questions posed for faith
> by the fact of historical flux, but to insist that an acknowledgement
> of the historical contingency of much of Christian teaching and
> institutions was compatible with firmly held orthodox belief, with
> the acceptance of dogma. . . .
>
> The doctrines of Incarnation and Trinity, accepted as fundamental
> by Catholics and Protestants, were not to be found in their mature
> form in the early church. And if the central tenets of faith could
> develop legitimately beyond their New Testament foundations,
> why not everything else?[63]

Newman realized: "Ideas must unfold in the historical process before
we can appropriate all they contain. So, beliefs evolve and change, but they
do so to preserve their essence in the flux of history."[64]

Our examination of the history of the Second Vatican Council on development and our concise summary of the teaching of cardinal Newman
on doctrinal development remind us that change is part of the spiritual
journey of the churches as they come together.[65]

62. Duffy, *John Henry Newman*, 3. When Newman was named a cardinal by the
Catholic Church, he took his motto from Saint Francis de Sales, "Heart speaks to Heart."

63. Duffy, *John Henry Newman*. 11.

64. Duffy, *John Henry Newman*, 12. Duffy offers this succinct overview of Newman's
thinking: "Newman combined a life-long insistence on the reliability of revealed truth—
of dogma—with a vivid awareness of the contingency of all Christian understanding and
utterance, even the most solemn creeds. In his consequent exploration of the legitimacy
of the development of doctrine; in his rejection of a narrow enlightenment understanding of rationality; in his recognition of the puzzle and difficulty of belief in God while
simultaneously defending the reasonableness of religious commitment; in his understanding the dynamic nature of the institutional church" (22). Newman explored many
topics still alive today.

65. For more on doctrinal development, see Clifford, "Reform and the Development
of Doctrine," 35–58. Francis, *Let Us Dream*, 57, remarks: "Tradition is not a museum,
true religion is not a freezer, and doctrine is not static but grows and develops, like a tree
that remains the same, yet which gets bigger and bears ever more fruit. There are some
who claim that God spoke once and for all time—almost always exclusively in the way
and the form that those who make this claim know well. They hear the work 'discernment' and worry that it is a fancy way of ignoring the rules or some clever modern ruse
to downgrade the truth when it is quite the opposite. Discernment is as old as the church.

In conclusion, it is worth noting that not only have the Christian churches seen development in the nineteen reflections on moral issues mentioned above, but the signatories of *JDDJ* have also seen changes in the ways they make moral decisions. American Methodists, for example, have moved from an early emphasis on the bishop to a more communal model. James Keenan notes that in the pre-Vatican II era, Catholics moved from referring to the "approved authors" for moral guidance to an emphasis on Papal teaching.

Crossin's Moral Paradigm Proposal

I am proposing that some of the signatories of JDDJ sponsor a Working Group that seeks to construct a common moral paradigm. This suggestion is a move forward from "this is how our Christian tradition makes moral decisions" to "these are the gift(s) of the Spirit that we have to contribute to a common moral framework." It is time to move into the future and not be paralyzed by some current disagreements.

I have proposed in this volume that such a paradigm might be built on the ten pillars which I elaborated in the chapters and which are mentioned in the Introduction and again in the appendix. These foundational elements need more development. This would be the task of the Working Group.

Such a paradigm might call for moral development—a change or nuance to moral teaching—but also a change in methods of authoritative approval. Examination of the Faith and Order studies considered above and of the churches' histories since the Reformation indicate that such change in content or method of approval is not unprecedented. But here we should note that the context has changed.

We are in the context of the world church. The presuppositions of European/North American theologies cannot be taken for granted. Thus, in this volume I have proposed spiritual, pastoral, biblical and relational foundations and in general have avoided presupposing the Greek philosophy which is not a common denominator in a world church.

A second change in context is that Christian ethics itself has become more complex. There is a need for individuals to engage in dialogue who

---

It follows from the promise Jesus made to his disciples that after he was gone the Spirit 'will guide you into all the truth' (John 16:13). There is no contradiction between being solidly rooted in the truth and at the same time being open to greater understanding."

have expertise in the many fields—such as psychology, neurobiology, scripture, and ecclesiology—that we have mentioned in this volume.

I believe that the foundations for a paradigm presented in this volume can be developed further. For example, the interrelationship of the ten foundational elements I proposed can be explored more thoroughly. They can be better integrated. Once this is accomplished, there will be ongoing refinements as with any paradigm. As mentioned previously, such a paradigm would provide common starting points for considering newer moral issues or revisiting older ones. These foundations could lead to common conclusions based on some common starting points and analysis of the issue in question. On the other hand, as I will reiterate in chapter 10, in a world church with billion(s) of Christians in communion with one another there will always be tensions to be endured and (hopefully) eventually synthesized.

Such a paradigm may also be of assistance to those now struggling with disagreements. The "Tool" developed by the Faith and Order Commission of the World Council of Churches should be of prime importance in helping those who disagree on moral teaching to come to mutual understanding.[66]

I believe that if a Working Group were to flesh out a Common Paradigm, it could help toward reconciliation. For example, if those who use the Faith and Order Commissions' "Tool" still diverge, perhaps a shift to a Common Paradigm would lead toward convergence as different presuppositions can lead to different moral insights.

We come now to the closing chapter where we will continue to reflect on the foundational elements for a common paradigm.

66. We will explain certain aspects of the "Tool" in chapter 10.

An Ecumenical Paradigm
for Moral Teaching

A Constructive Proposal

MY HOPE IN WRITING this book is to lay groundwork for developing an ecumenical ethical paradigm that will guide Christian communities as they move toward full communion. The long-term goal is to have a common framework to help us. We need a clear and deeply rooted moral paradigm that assists us in spreading the gospel.

In this chapter, we will present many of the significant elements in this ecumenical paradigm: biblical teaching, fundamental sacraments, future orientation, the Faith and Order "Tool" which can help dissonant voices come to mutual understanding, the ten foundational elements, and some ways to look at issues—differentiated consensus, accepting tensions in the church, and dealing with a human tendency to universalize our personal experience. All these are parts of the ongoing development of an ethical paradigm.

We begin this chapter with reference to the account of Jesus post-resurrection appearance to the two disciples on the "Road to Emmaus." The full text is Luke 24:13–35.

This potent passage gives us a great deal of guidance in discerning an ecumenical paradigm. (1) Jesus is walking with and speaking with us, but we may not recognize him. We can be preoccupied, as were the disciples on the road, with difficulties (and differences) rather than with positive possibilities. (2) Jesus and the Holy Spirit speak to us of the meaning of the Scriptures for Christian ethics. (3) Are we distracted in our conversation by our emotional response to the current situation? (4) Have we noticed if our hearts are burning within us? (5) Will our eyes be opened in the breaking/ sharing of the bread?

Jesus disappears at the end—returning to the Father.[1] Our good news from the resurrected Jesus is to be shared. The two disciples' emotions have changed from sorrowful to joyful. They were returning home, separating themselves from the other disciples. Now they are returning to Jerusalem and rejoining the others. Will we do the same and rejoin one another?[2]

We will need to be aware of our emotional reactions as we discuss moral paradigms and moral issues. Joy and peace are characteristic of the Spirit. The eucharistic celebration may be a decisive moment in recognizing Jesus and the Holy Spirit in our midst.

Biblical scholar Gerhard Lohfink considers this appearance on the road to Emmaus as exemplary of Jesus' post-resurrection appearances.[3] Lohfink goes on to discuss the "new creation." This new life in Christ begins with baptism and is nourished in the Eucharist and reconciliation. "Both creation and resurrection are pure gift and connected."[4]

Furthermore, "The New Testament contains a tension between what theologians call 'already' and 'not yet.' Christian eschatology is in tension between the 'already' of the salvation that has come and the 'not yet' of completed salvation, and that 'already' is happening, unceasingly, in this history. . . . The 'last things' for humans have already begun in the existence of the baptized."[5]

Scripture scholar Francis J. Moloney, SDB, notes in his commentary on John's Gospel that the "blood and water" that flowed from Jesus' side (19:31–34) indicates that after Jesus had "entrusted the Spirit to the

---

1. We recall from earlier chapters that there is an underlying Trinitarian emphasis in *JDDJ*, in receptive ecumenism, in spiritual ecumenism/discernment, and in the Eucharist.

2. For interesting reflections on this passage, see Koch, "What Model of Full Communion?," 605–6. For my reflections on this essay and others, see Crossin, "Will Christian Unity Come Sooner?," 18–23.

3. Lohfink, *Is This All There Is?*, 114. See Moloney, *Eucharist as a Celebration of Forgiveness*.

4. Lohfink, *Is This All There Is?*, 127.

5. Lohfink, *Is This All There Is?*, 250–51.

community (v. 30), now he entrusts the blood and water of Eucharist and Baptism."[6] This points to the continuity between Christ and the community of disciples. This continuity was seen as the work of the Spirit and as involving the two primary sacraments even at the time John's Gospel was written.[7]

Dennis Billy, in his chapter "Contemplating Jesus Resurrection," affirms the importance of baptism and the Eucharist and goes on to say: "Jesus' Resurrection has much to tell us about the Christian spiritual moral life. It reminds us of our destiny in God and that Jesus is the way to get there. . . . Jesus' message is spread primarily through the witness of saintly lives, of people who are thoroughly committed to following their Lord."[8]

Lohfink, Moloney and Billy all point to the importance of the early Christian communities and their continuity with the risen Christ through baptism and Eucharist. I infer from this that our work in ecumenical ethics, while having an individual component, is also communal and while having a "look back" also "looks forward" with the assistance of the Holy Spirit.

The Fundamental Sacraments: Baptism and Eucharist

The Finnish Lutheran-Catholic dialogue it its 2017 statement offered a detailed study of sacraments and agreed that baptism and Eucharist are the central sacraments in the Church. "We agree that the Eucharist is the *centre* of the Church's life. Both the individual person and the Church gain their spiritual life and strength from the Eucharist. Participation in the Mass is the basic model for Christian living. Baptism incorporates the baptized into the body of Christ and the Eucharist helps him or her to mature and grow therein" (no. 93). The dialogue addressed remaining issues and stated that "a joint declaration on the Church, Eucharist, and Ministry is needed as the next step" (no. 367). I believe that this would be a momentous step.

Paul McPartlan, reflecting on the ancient tradition, speaks of the Eucharist as embracing both past and future. The Last Supper and the Eternal Banquet are evident in the present eucharistic moment. All the angels and saints (Catholic, Protestant, Orthodox, and others) are present.[9]

The Holy Spirit will gift us with deeper insight into our moral teachings through the Word, sacrament, gathered community, and its presider as

6. Moloney, *The Gospel of John*, 505.

7. See Finnish Lutheran Catholic Dialogue, "Communion in Growth," nos. 63–71.

8. Billy, *Contemplative Ethics*, 132–33.

9. McPartlan, *Sacrament of Salvation*, 4–5.

we pray together at the Eucharist/Lord's Supper.[10] Our prayer together can both flow from and lead to deeper contemplation.

In the prayerful contemplative context encouraged by Dennis Billy, we might listen to and pray over the findings of modern science referred to earlier in this volume and the reflections on these findings by contemporary Christians. A major participant in such meditation/contemplation was Teilhard de Chardin.[11] In sketching out a moral trajectory of life, Teilhard's considerations would be for the morally mature.[12]

Preliminaries

I will not review my reflections and ruminations on the important documents elaborated on in chapter 9 other than to say that they offer ample material for constructing a more detailed ecumenical ethical paradigm. Drawing on my remarks in chapter 9, I would stress: that it is important for dialogue members who are working on such a paradigm to get to know one another; that Scripture is central but tradition, reason, and experience also have an important role; that some common criteria for communal discernment are necessary; and that the charism of authority calls on leaders to make decisions toward unity in a timely fashion.

I might begin by mentioning that construction of a paradigm is not like the legislative process we see in Washington, DC, and in state capitols where legislators can compromise and get part of what they want. In seeking to build a moral paradigm we are listening for the "tiny whispering sound" by which the Spirit guides us in ways we would never have expected. What is God's will for us is the best! Our best attitude is one of gratitude to God.

It is important to note that the virtue paradigm that I am advocating has a positive emphasis. That is, Christians are to grow in love for God and for neighbor. The divine love poured into our hearts by the Holy Spirit transforms our natural virtues and directs us toward doing the good. With

10. See F&O, *Facilitating Dialogue*, ix: "This document . . . provides ways of deepening understanding, of entering into dialogue with calmness and confidence, and of strengthening communion between and within our churches."

11. See Duffy, *Teilhard's Mysticism*.

12. See Gibbs, *Moral Development and Reality*, 106. In his book *Teilhard de Chardin on Morality*, noted scholar Louis M. Savary summarizes the eight Basic Principles of Teilhard's thought and Teilhard's eleven Moral Principles related to these Basics. Savary discusses each of the Basic Principles of Thought and each of the Moral Principles.

divine assistance, Christians can grow in loving as summarized by Francis de Sales in his four stages of loving mentioned in chapter 7.

The ethical life is about doing the good, not just about avoiding evil, though avoiding evil is a necessary aspect of ethics given the human condition. Thus, as mentioned previously, we are receiving "a wakeup call" if we realize we are getting close to or going past the boundaries set by the Ten Commandments.

The virtuous life is about doing the good. A prime spiritual question we might be asking ourselves is: "How can I turn this particular situation to the good?" or "How might I use the gifts God has given me to make this bad situation better (which is not to say perfect)?" The overall context is positive, though not without the caution just mentioned about our human weaknesses/sinfulness.

There are other issues beyond the ten foundations that must be addressed if alternative moral paradigms to VE arise in the world church. Thus, for example, what would be a hermeneutic that would relate the biblical teaching to contemporary moral issues; or what philosophical resources would be operative within the paradigm; and what would be the balance between individual and communal decision making in the cultural world of the paradigm?

What is of concern at this moment to the ecumenically minded Christian churches is the already-existing difference on moral issues that are causing divisions within and between the churches. These divisions are increasing our cacophony to the ears of outsiders and insiders. These divisions make sharing our faith with outsiders more difficult. The Faith and Order Commission's third document in 2021 entitled *Facilitating Dialogue to Build Koinonia* addresses this concern and offers a "Tool" to help clarify or even to help integrate the differences.

What follows is a concise overview of salient points of this document.

Moving towards Consensus, Facilitating Dialogue to Build Koinonia[13]

The Introduction to this document embraces many points that we have mentioned in this book such as: the relationship between continuity and change is not always linear (no. 1); our common commitment as Christians

---

13. I am indebted to World Council of Churches Publications for their permission to quote this important document extensively.

to a moral life of loving God and neighbor (no. 2); the way/church as a community of pilgrims (no. 4); specific virtues as characterizing the way (no. 4); the moral life as a communal not just an individual commitment (no. 5); the unique worth and dignity of every human being (no. 8); our everyday loving actions (Matt 25:31–46) as well as our liturgical actions make the reign of God present in history (no. 10); and the need to increase dialogue based on our common ground to deal with our divergences. (no. 16)

We will examine *three important elements* of this text while acknowledging that there are many other elements worthy of prayerful study.

First, we should mention that we count very much on people's sincerity even though it does not mean we will agree on a given issue (no. 23). What is/are the moral process(es) that led to the current or proposed moral norms? We assume that this process is grounded in our mutual attempts to be faithful to the gospel (no. 23). Does the process involve different predispositions to continuity and change? We are seeking consensus.

Secondly, the text defines the *conscience of the church* (nos. 24–26). The *conscience of the church* involves the whole community.

> This study uses the term "conscience of the church" to refer to this dynamic corporate engagement of a church with the moral challenges it confronts—analogous with how, in many traditions, the individual believer engages with moral challenges through their conscience. *The Church Towards a Common Vision* describes the whole community as involved in this corporate engagement. (no. 25)

> In this study, the term "conscience of the church" is a term for how all these sources [guidance of the Holy Spirit, scripture, tradition, teaching and decision-making authority, spirituality, church culture, and lived experience] are at work in the dynamic activity of the body of Christ that believes it is being guided by the Holy Spirit. (no. 26)

Chapter 2 in *Facilitating Dialogue to Build Koinonia* explores the meaning of the "conscience of the church" at some length. The chapter has a good summary of the varied reactions to historical situations:

> Some of these reactions consist of a firm reiteration of a church's position; some . . . include accommodation of a particular situation at the pastoral level . . . ; some include development in the understanding of an existing position, affecting its application without altering its existence; some . . . may even lead to changes

or modification of practice or moral teaching and the abandon-
ment or even condemnation of the previous position. (no. 40)

We should note that this emphasis on the conscience of the church
restores a healthy balance between the individual and the community.
Facilitating Dialogue seeks a balance between individual freedom and the
moral community.

Chapter 3 speaks of how "Changes Emerge" and gives examples (no.
63). A salient question the chapter raises for us is: "How can churches, despite a plurality of views on some issues, come to affirm their common
convictions on so many issues rooted in the conscience of the church?"
(no. 64).

Thirdly, the fourth chapter offers "A Tool to Understand Disagreement
and Facilitate Dialogue to Build Koinonia."

The chapter gives a detailed exposition with examples of the "Tool"
that the Faith and Order Commission has developed. It is necessary to read
and pray over this chapter thoroughly. The "Tool" will be quite significant
if accepted and put into practice. What follows are some highlights of this
chapter and some comments on their relationship to a common moral
paradigm.

   a. The Commission notes that *The Church: Towards a Common Vision*
      in para. 24 invites the churches "to reflect together about the criteria
      which are employed in different churches for considering issues about
      continuity and change" (no. 68). If we are to work together to build
      a common moral paradigm, continuity and change will be a central
      consideration. We might note here that an individual's capacity to deal
      with change is related to his/her stage of moral development.[14]

   b. The Commission mentions that the "Tool" is not merely "for discerning
      differences" but also can lead to joint action by Christian communities.
      We might emphasize the importance of common action for the good of
      society as well as for the good of the Christian churches. (no. 69)

   c. We might note here that in building a common paradigm we are called
      to incorporate the gifts for moral discernment given by the Spirit to
      each of the traditions who are in dialogue. (cf. no. 70)

   d. The Commission considers that its most important recommenda-
      tion coming from its six years of work is: "Affirmation of the value of

14. See Gibbs' citation in the footnote above.

131

engaging in structured dialogues about the process of moral discernment." (no. 71)[15]

e. The Commission says that part of the challenge is distinguishing legitimate diversity. They also mention that in every change there are elements that remain unchanged. (no. 74)

The Commission gives a detailed explanation of the "Tool": (1) the *conscience of the church* engages context; and (2) the *conscience of the church*—and thus the "Tool"—has four elements each of which plays a role in moral discernment: moral norms, ecclesial understanding of authority and purpose of discourse, ecclesial conception of salvation history and ecclesial identity, and disposition to change. "The tool helps dialogue partners make explicit what is often implicit in dialogue on moral discernment" (nos. 86–88).

Furthermore, "Each of the four elements has a corresponding range of "positions" or "types" that go from typically more stable (i.e., less prone to change in response to changes in circumstances) to more contingent (i.e., more susceptible or likely to change in response to circumstances.)" (no. 90).

Reflections

In its conclusion, the Commission summarizes saying "The study document, therefore, offers a tool to better understand the different factors that play a role in the way the conscience of the church is understood and how it affects the moral discernment process." They offer a helpful "Appendix: Guiding Questions to Use of the Tool."

Facilitating Dialogue to Build Koinonia offers possibilities for a deeper understanding of convergences and differences on moral issues between and within Christian traditions. It sees a process rooted in Christian commitment, prayer, and discernment of the guidance of the Spirit. Its emphasis falls much more on norms than on virtues. Its focus is on moral contradictions in the present moment. It does not offer a systematic approach to engaging future issues—though it might be helpful in doing so.

Facilitating Dialogue also does not mention the assistance of a spiritual guide in discernment. For example, the role of the spiritual guide in helping members of Orthodox churches in the exercise of balancing of *akriveia* and *oikonomia* in individual cases (nos. 38–39) is missing.

---

15. Section 71 found on p. 48 is worth study beyond what is possible here.

The "Tool" just discussed is a most welcome addition which can help bring Christian communities closer together or even to agreement on controverted issues.

Elements for a Moral Paradigm—Sermon on the Mount

Our extended discussion of paradigms in chapter 6 gives the background for our reflection on moral paradigms. The word paradigm itself suggests that change, though difficult, can take place in moral thinking over time. It also suggests relationships and a system. Early Christians such as Irenaeus sought to develop systematic approaches to Christian teaching. How can we be consistent with what Jesus taught? Our contemporary discussions can tend to focus on single moral issues as if they were independent from other issues. A paradigm reminds us of the interconnections of issues within Christian morality.

Another advantage in speaking in terms of paradigms is that paradigms can change gradually as new thinking is integrated with old but occasionally can change dramatically based on some central insight that affects all or most of the important moral questions.

As mentioned in our introduction, we identify ten important items that we contend are part of moral paradigms. These are listed again in the appendix with questions for consideration. The chapters listed with the questions provide deeper insights into these items and encourage further consideration of them.

The four major scriptural elements for any moral paradigm: *the Sermon on the Mount, the commandments to love God and neighbor, the Ten Commandments, and the works of mercy (Matt 25:31–46)* cohere well with the word and example of the earliest Christians and Christians down through the centuries to our own time.[16] This emphasis on Scriptural teaching also coheres well with the emphasis of the *JDDJ*.

The Sermon on the Mount has been historically and is still today the central element in Jesus moral teaching. In beginning his discussion of the Sermon, Daniel Harrington says "The history of the sermon's interpretation is a miniature history of Christianity. To the present day there are sharply conflicting approaches to it."[17]

---

16. See chapter 3 above.

17. Harrington, *The Gospel of Matthew*, 76.

Noted ethicist Glen Stassen in his concise reflection on the Sermon on the Mount begins with some cautions about "Ways of Interpreting that Lead to Evasion." He mentions (1) *Literal Interpretation applied universally and absolutely*—Stassen believes that such interpretations of the 'never be angry' type discourage practice of Jesus's teaching by making it seem impossible. (2) *Hyperbole*—He believes that while Jesus does teach by hyperbole at times this does not mean his teaching should not be taken seriously. (3) *General Principles*—Stassen believes that what Jesus taught, for example in carrying a Roman soldier's pack an extra mile, should be applied today and "take concrete shape in our historical context." (4) Double Standard— the teaching of Jesus is not for a select group of Christians only [such as vowed religious order members] but are to be lived by all Christians.[18] (5) *Repentance*—Christians are to repent when they violate the teaching of Jesus rather than say the Sermon does not apply to me! And (6) *Interim Ethic*—Here the point is that Jesus teaching applies now and not just in a future kingdom.[19]

Harrington has five main elements in his approach to the Sermon itself. "(1) Matthew places Jesus' teaching in an eschatological framework (see 5:3–12; 7:13–27)" even though Jesus' teaching is about behavior in the present. "(2) The sermon is neither a strictly individual ethic nor a blueprint for social Utopia." Yet it has implications for both social and individual life. (3) The sermon is not for a social elite nor is it impossible to practice. (4) "The sermon places a compendium of Jesus' teachings before Jews primarily." This is to show Jesus fulfills the Law and the Prophets. "(5) In it, Jesus presents what is for Christians an authoritative interpretation of the Torah." Here Jesus is concerned more with principles than with laws.[20]

We should note at this point that we argued earlier in this volume that a virtue approach sublates (includes but transforms) an emphasis on justice and the law. Pertinent examples include Schockenhoff's views on Natural Law and Gibbs' views on moral development both of which were mentioned earlier in our text.[21]

We have reviewed the Faith and Order Commissions tool for considering divergences on moral issues, referred to the ten foundations for an

---

18. It is sometimes forgotten that Saint Francis de Sales articulated this point of view in his *Introduction to the Devout Life* over five hundred years ago.

19. Stassen, "Sermon on the Mount," 715–16.

20. Harrington, *The Gospel of Matthew*, 76.

21. See chapters 6 and 7, respectively.

Ecumenical Ethical Paradigm, and discussed the Sermon on the Mount as the central biblical moral teaching which grounds an Ecumenical Ethic of virtue. As noted earlier, Christians will still have some divergences on moral issues. We now consider how we might categorize moral issues.

Categorizing Moral Issues

Christians agree completely on many moral issues. Further ecumenical considerations moving Christian communities toward moral consensus on divisive issues would include looking at them through different lenses. Some differences may be amenable to a differentiated consensus; others present polarities that must be maintained in tension though perhaps they will eventually lead to new syntheses; and tendencies to "Universalizing one's personal experience" might best lead to pastoral directives from a local synod on wise pastoral approaches that limit overgeneralization.

A. The Joint Declaration—Differentiated Consensus

Recent ecumenical convergences shed some light on the convergences and divergences on moral questions as we come closer to full communion. We learn quite a bit from the *JDDJ*'s method of differentiated consensus and its use in the Finnish Lutheran-Catholic Dialogue we discussed earlier.

1. We do not need agreement on all moral issues just as *JDDJ* did not propose agreement on every single aspect of justification discussed by theologians over the centuries.

2. Our common foundations are in Scripture. *JDDJ* affirms newer methods of discovering the meaning of Scripture such as the historical-critical method for the world behind the text and narrative criticism which considers both the author and the reader in front of the text.[22]

3. The importance of the trinitarian foundation to the *JDDJ* and the work on ecumenical ethics should not be underestimated. We will seek to imitate the words and example of Jesus who is at one with the Father and who sends us the Paraclete.[23]

22. See Moloney, *The Gospel of John*, 13–20.

23. See Moloney, *Love in the Gospel of John*, 37–69. Moloney considers Jesus's relationship to and mission from the Father as presented in John's Gospel. The Father loves the Son and shows his love for the universe and for humanity by sending the Son.

4. The Christian's active love is enabled by the Holy Spirit.

5. Jesus dying on the Cross gave up his Spirit (John 19:30b): "Now the Spirit is poured out. If the seamless robe was a symbol of the community of disciples and the gift of the Mother to Son and Son to Mother foreshadowed the unity of faith, faith that is the *ekklesia* of God . . . then it is upon the nascent community that the Spirit is poured."[24] This community is a social ethic.

These citations also remind us of the history of Christian ethics which indicates that there have been changes over time in Christian moral teaching such as that on usury. Might we say that there exists a differentiated consensus on usury given the fact that, as the three essays on usury in Volume 2 of the Faith and Order Commission come to similar conclusions but by different paths?[25] Might we speak of a differentiated consensus on other issues?

B. Polarities and Synodality

Full communion between Catholics and Protestants and Orthodox, our ecumenical vision, might include 80 percent of all Christians.[26] This is well over a billion people. It would be naive to think there will not be differences of opinion and tensions.

The differences/tensions between those who hold to capital punishment and those who would eliminate it; between those who follow just war thinking and those who promote pacifism; or between those Catholics who support artificial means of contraception and those who do not point to a Christian ethics with some diversity of opinion.[27]

24. Moloney, *The Gospel of John*, 504–5.

25. F&O, *Learning from History*, 1–49.

26. I contend elsewhere that I believe for various good reasons—e.g., discernment of God's will, community obligations—not all Christians will come into full communion. This discernment should be respected.

27. For a discussion of the Catholic debate on contraception, see Keenan, *A History of Catholic Moral Theology*, chapter 6, "The Neo-Manualists," and chapter 7, "New Foundations for Moral Reasoning, 1970–89." These two chapters include discussions on Pope Paul VI's encyclical *Humanae vitae*, Pope John Paul's encyclical *Veritatis splendor*, and the rise again of the consideration of moral cases (casuistry) as an important dimension of moral theology. The chapters are amply footnoted. Mark Massa, in his *The Structure of Theological Revolutions*, chapter 3 "A Period of Crisis," and chapter 5, "Germain Grisez and the New Natural Law," "offers a historian's view of the *Humanae Vitae* controversy and of the New Natural Law." William E. May, who supports the New Natural Law

These remind us, as discussed earlier in this book, that Pope Francis speaks of the polarities within the Christian community.[28]

> Bergoglio's "dialogical thinking" does not represent . . . an irenic solution defined by easy optimism but the result of ontological reflection. *The ontology of polarity requires dialogical thinking, directed toward a synthetic horizon, that resists a "contradictory" interpretation of its poles.* The framework is that of a "catholic" thought that understands the church and life as a *complexio oppositorum*, an agonizing struggle to overcome conflicts, to prevent the resolution of polarities into Manichean contradictions. The thought has its root in the mystery of the church.

Pope Francis discussion of polarities, which draws from the work of Romano Guardini, speaks of contradictions which can lead to divisions and tensions that can lead to new syntheses.

One danger here is that groups will withdraw into circles of perceived safety and ignore the Spirit's guidance. Rather, one should emphasize the tensions within the church that force us to get out of ourselves and our worlds and encounter other Christians, learn from them, and become holy. There will always be tensions between pastoral and academic theology, between different schools of thought—such as Thomist or Franciscan—and different points of view. New syntheses may develop just as Francis de Sales brought together Jesuit, Thomistic, Franciscan, Carmelite, and other points of view into his own characteristically gentle and respectful way of thinking and acting.

Pope Francis's "dialogical thinking" is evident in his stance on "gay marriage." He maintains the church teaching while encouraging pastoral outreach and concern for "gay couples." He seems to be waiting for a synthetic moment to come out of the tension. In this electronic age, one of instant "solutions," the patience and perseverance necessary for a synthesis to emerge may not be present easily. However, we should not underestimate the possibility that saints might be present to show us the way.

---

paradigm, gives an extended explication of it in his *An Introduction to Moral Theology.* For an interesting and helpful alternative see M. John Farrelly, OSB, "Contraception as a Test Case for the Development of Doctrine," 453–72. His concept of the "marital good" encompassing the whole set of relationships in the family is key to his moderate realism. While his position did not gain traction in the heated debate over *Humanae vitae*, it may be helpful in a paradigm that prioritizes relationships.

28. Summarizing and quoting Borghesi, "The Polarity Model," 135, and the initial explanation in chapter 5 of this book.

In his book *Let Us Dream*, Pope Francis devotes some pages to renewing the ancient practice of synodality.[29] He speaks of the "productive tension of "walking together" whether in the church or in civil society. We seek the truth while recognizing the richness of our polarities and with the patience necessary in seeking to learn from one another and in accepting a good synthesis if one develops. Synodality is essential to our ongoing dialogue about controverted moral issues. While we agree:

- to our common biblical roots in the Sermon on the Mount, love of God and neighbor, the Ten Commandments, and practice of the works of mercy, and

- while we have noted elements of a differentiated consensus,

- we realize that new moral issues continue to arise and

- that a synodal process is necessary for churches in full communion to discuss emerging or reemerging moral issues.[30]

A synodal process relies on participation and the guidance of the Spirit. We recall that God is a God of surprises and so we work, pray, and walk together.

C. Universalizing

In my pastoral work, I see the tendency to universalize. A salient example is a woman I knew at a nearby parish. She went on a retreat and came back overflowing with joy over her spiritual encounter with Christ. She spoke with me because she was extremely disappointed that others with whom she shared her experience were not similarly enthused. We talked and I eventually suggested that she had received a special grace and others had not—or God had spoken to them in some other way. She universalized her own experience—everyone should feel/be the way she felt.

There can be a tendency to generalize one's personal or communal experience or one's moral insight and say it should be applied to all Christians! All Christians is an exceptionally large number of people in today's world church. It seems to me that such human tendencies should

---

29. For a concise, helpful overview of synodality, see Mayer, "For a Synodal Church," 205–14.

30. Francis, *Let Us Dream*, 81–83.

be addressed at a local or regional level perhaps through the efforts of a local ecumenical synod.

We thus can look at moral issues: as ones where Christians agree; or as ones where there is a differentiated consensus; or as ones where there is tensive opposition, perhaps capable of eventual synthesis; or as ones which are local or regional; or as ones where divergence is possible, even likely, and acceptable—such as how to handle migration and immigration considering love for neighbor and Jesus's example.

An Exploratory Work

This concluding chapter is as much exploratory as definitive. As with other parts of this text I am seeking to contribute to what I perceive will be an ongoing discussion of Christian ethics—even after churches come into full communion. Many moral issues and perspectives change over time. Some of this happens quickly as for example in questions related to biomedical ethics. Other questions unfold more slowly such as questions as to whether there is a natural law and whether it or our perception of it changes with new understandings or paradigms.

Of particular interest, given the reflections above, is the impact of Virtue Ethics. Many Catholic, Protestant, and Orthodox ethicists embrace VE. A particularly perspicuous new approach to virtuous actions is the work of David Cloutier and Anthony H. Ahrens on moral agency. "The authors suggest social cognitive theory provides key insights into the mechanics of agents 'acting from character' and offers an empirical program that can further our understanding of moral disagreement."[31] They integrate the insights of Social Cognitive Theory (SCT) into consideration of virtuous action in order to develop a theory of "how virtue works."

In their quite detailed explanation, the authors

> suggest a model of virtuous practical rationality that integrates important elements of SCT with the "standard model" largely indebted to Aquinas. This "interactional" model of virtue enhances the standard model, especially by offering new insights on the

---

31. Cloutier and Ahrens, "Catholic Moral Theology and the Virtues," 326. The footnotes cite numerous resources for those who wish to follow some recent developments in Virtue Ethics.

relations between reason and the passions (or emotions), on the notion of practical reasoning itself, and on the idea of the will.[32]

The emphasis of SCT on both cognition and on social context should satisfy many moralists.[33] This model emphasizes an interaction between the person and the situation. Cloutier and Ahrens contend that the emphasis should fall of the "dynamic nature" of a person's dispositions which cannot really be specified apart from "interactional instantiations."[34] Their model, which we only considered briefly, thus rejects reason-feeling dichotomies, and emphasizes that phronesis (practical wisdom, prudence) "is a central feature of every virtue."[35]

The authors stay in touch with classical views of action but develop a theory of virtuous action that is highly distinctive as well. My intuition is that this development of the elements of a virtuous moral act could offer a way forward on some disagreements. The authors offer a contemporary, integrated, developmental and experiential approach that could assist the considerations summarized in this chapter. The authors recent essay reminds us that Christian ethics is a dynamic field. It will continue to change as scholars and pastors come to new insights into Christian moral action.

Saint Francis de Sales mentions that in the spiritual life we are always either going backwards or going forwards. There is always motion though sometimes it is subtle. There is a similar "on the way" dimension to Christian ethics and to the development of an ecumenical ethical paradigm. We live in a dynamic universe and at times we wish that life was a little more static. We want things settled finally! Likewise, we can want our Christian ethics to be all black and white and are chagrined that some of our moral decisions are in the "gray area." In this area, which encompasses a significant part of everyday life, we may want absolute certainty in our moral decisions instead of *the relative certainty* that is possible.

---

32. Cloutier and Ahrens, "Catholic Moral Theology and the Virtues," 328.

33. Cloutier and Ahrens, "Catholic Moral Theology and the Virtues," 334.

34. Cloutier and Ahrens, "Catholic Moral Theology and the Virtues," 336.

35. Cloutier and Ahrens, "Catholic Moral Theology and the Virtues," 342. See chapter 4 on the importance of prudence.

Final Reflection

My hope in writing this chapter is that we can begin to see more clearly the outlines of a moral paradigm that integrates both norms and virtues. We have many elements but not the total framework.

What I suggest would be an international group of moralists that needs to address the question of (a) common moral paradigms and related issues. Christian ethics today is complicated and no one person has expertise in all its dimensions. Christian ethics today calls for a team. Works such as this book are beginnings not endings.

As I did earlier in this volume, I do take stances on some central issues. I list elements for a moral paradigm and believe that biblical teaching and especially the four major moral elements listed earlier in this chapter take center stage in an ecumenical ethics. These can only be understood, of course, in the context of the entire gospel message as, for example, the encounter of the two disciples with Jesus walking on the road to Emmaus. An ecumenical ethics will be future oriented. After Jesus left, the two disciples changed directions. Instead of going back home, they went up to Jerusalem to share with the others their encounter with Jesus and to share the road ahead.

Appendix

Preparing for Dialogue

The Preliminaries

THE PREPARATION FOR DIALOGUE about moral foundations is in daily prayer. "The foundational principle of spiritual ecumenism is that the more Christians live holier lives according to the gospel, the better they will practice Christian unity, for the closer their union to Father, Word, and Spirit, the more deeply they will be able to grow in mutual love."[1]

Dennis Billy develops this insight of the Second Vatican Council in his "Guidelines for Christian Living" in *Contemplative Ethics: An Introduction*. He believes that we can also elicit a "number of guidelines, all of which are interrelated and uniquely oriented toward the telos of the spiritual moral life in the new creation."[2] The Spirit might lead a participant in a dialogue on ecumenical ethics to pray over one or several of the following:

We search out stillness.

We engage in active listening.

We value and form right relationships.

We act as mediators.

We foster communication at various levels.

1. Vatican Council II, "Decree on Ecumenism," no. 7, in Wood and Wengert, "The Path," 41.

2. Billy, *Contemplative Ethics*, 39.

We seek to heal and transform.

We live in the service of others.

We empathize with others and are involved in their lives.

We act out of love for others.

We are committed to building up the kingdom.

Finally, we bring our actions to prayer.[3]

Billy contends that for these guidelines to have any lasting effect, they must themselves be meditated upon and internalized so that they might become deeply rooted in our conscious thought patterns and decision-making processes. Such internalization takes place most effectively when we open our hearts in quiet prayer and ponder the mysteries of God's Eternal Word in a dynamic relationship of reciprocal care and loving concern.[4]

> The Eternal Word is distinct from the Father and the Spirit by virtue of its relationship to them. The Word cannot and does not exist outside of right relationship. In like manner, we must place the formation of right relationships at the forefront of our ethical concerns. To do so, we must be willing to examine the dysfunctional ways in which we related (to ourselves, each other, institutions, the environment, God) and try to find ways of alleviating the tensions we find in our relationships. The goal we should be working toward is to have the relationships within the Trinity increasingly reflected in those we forge with others.[5]

Of course, ecumenical dialogues thrive if the participants are women and men of deep prayer.

A second resource for reflection/contemplation are materials provided before the meeting. We must also pray over our own contribution. An inventory of one's personal experiences of the questions being discussed and of one's emotional reactions to them would be helpful as well as study of one's emotional reaction to other members' work.

---

3. Billy, *Contemplative Ethics*, 39–44. Billy elaborates on each of the guidelines individually as he lists them.

4. Billy, *Contemplative Ethics*, 46.

5. Billy, *Contemplative Ethics*, 40.

Personal and Communal Discernment

In this prayerful context, we might engage in personal and communal discernment. In the communal discernment, we seek the guidance of the Spirit both in our individual preparation and as we share communally.[6]

The history of Christian spirituality presents us with numerous criteria for personal discernment. Personal discernments become part of the process of communal discernment necessary to develop a robust paradigm.

As mentioned in detail in chapter 2, Francis de Sales offers criteria for personal discernment. He speaks of: God's signified will (e.g., the Ten Commandments, the Beatitudes); a communal process; freedom of spirit; perseverance in our vocation; affective states such as joy, peace, and consolation/desolation in prayer; and virtues such as humility, obedience, and charity in his discussions of discernment.[7]

Ladislas Orsy's concise book on communal discernment, while more attuned to practical discernment in local communities, offers an abundance of insights that might be helpful in discerning together a common moral paradigm. This include his insights that communal discernment requires: a long-term habit of prayer; contemplative insight; wisdom and being attuned to the Holy Spirit; awareness that communal discernment is part of Christian history; awareness of members' limitations; respect for the integrity of each person; and allowing enough time for deliberations.[8]

Prayerful preparation could include meeting with one's spiritual director for some discussion of these criteria for discernment.

Review of Foundations

A participant in dialogue about ecumenical ethics might take some time to review the basic elements of a moral paradigm mentioned in the Introduction to this book and how they might be evident in discussions and dialogue.

---

6. We have been advocating a pneumatological model. See Strong, *The Economy of the Spirit*, 1–7.

7. Crossin, *Walking in Virtue*, 67–70. Here I diverge somewhat from Dougherty, *Discernment*, 9–13, who stresses the role of experience over method for individuals. I think that a method of discernment sharing common criteria would be helpful to ecumenical dialogues though I realize that there is a need to balance criteria with personal experience.

8. Orsy, *Discernment*, 9–52.

Appendix

1. *A focus on ongoing conversion to Christ and the guidance of the Holy Spirit and the realization that we will never completely comprehend the mystery of the Trinity and can always grow in our understanding and practice of our Christian faith* (chapter 1)

    a. How have you seen/felt the guidance of the Spirit in your process of deliberation/discernment?
    b. Is there a Trinitarian dimension to your deliberations? To the construction of a paradigm?
    c. How has the teaching and example of Jesus influenced your thinking about questions/ norm/virtues under consideration?

2. *Concern for pastoral experience with a focus on the uniqueness of everyone made in God's image* (chapters 2 and 8)

    a. What pastoral experiences have been shared in the process of considering the issue/norm/virtue at hand?
    b. Is there social science data that a bear on the question under consideration? How is such data to be incorporated into a paradigm that is scriptural?

3. *Emphasis on discernment of God's will* (chapters 2 and 9)

    a. What method(s) of discerning God's will have you seen in your discussions?
    b. Where do you stand on discernment in comparison to your colleagues in dialogue and comparison with noted authors on ways to discern?

4. *A realization that a Christian ethic should rely on prayerful contemplation as much as rational arguments* (chapters 2, 4, and 10)

    a. Has the dialogue group devoted time to prayer?
    b. Has the group discussed the meaning of contemplation?
    c. Has the affective element in prayer influenced the dialogue?

5. *Reverence for and inclusion of our Jewish heritage especially the Old Testament and the realization that we interpret our Jewish heritage through the teaching of Jesus and the New Testament* (chapter 3)

    a. Has the work of Jewish scholars influenced the dialogue group's deliberations?
    b. Has Jewish interpretation of the OT affected your personal deliberations?

6. *The importance of relationships and the contributions of relational the-ologies* (chapter 4)

    a.   Has consideration been given to the importance of relationships with God, neighbor, and community in your discussion of moral paradigms?
    b.   Has consideration of relationships as above influenced your discussion of norms, cases, and virtues?

7. *The conclusions of formal ecumenical dialogues* (chapter 5)

    a.   How might the conclusions of (other) dialogues impact your own discussions and conclusions?

8. *Recognition that spiritual/moral growth goes through stages* (chapter 7)

    a.   What degree of spiritual maturity is necessary to live out this norm, virtue, teaching?
    b.   What level of spiritual maturity does this paradigm presuppose, if any.
    c.   Has Gibbs data on moral development had any influence on your considerations of paradigms and/or specifics.

9. *Deep understanding of Jesus' teaching, especially on the Sermon on the Mount, the commandments to love God and neighbor, the Ten Com-mandments, and the works of mercy (Matt 25:31–46)* (chapter 10)

    a.   How do these biblical teachings serve the building of a moral paradigm(s)?

10. *As much focus on Jesus' resurrection as on his suffering and death, on the Eternal Banquet as on the Last Supper* (chapter 10)

    a.   How prominent is the resurrection and the grace of the Spirit in your considerations?

Bibliography

Armstrong, John. *Costly Love: The Way to True Unity for All the Followers of Jesus*. Hyde Park, NY: New City, 2017.

Barr, Stephen M. *Modern Physics and Ancient Faith*. Notre Dame: University of Notre Dame Press, 2003.

Bartholomew I. "During Visit to National Council of Churches (USA) His All-Holiness Ecumenical Patriarch Bartholomew Urges We 'Must Change the Way We See the World and Society.'" *WCC*, November 4, 2021. https://www.oikoumene.org/news/during-visit-to-national-council-of-churches-usa-his-all-holiness-ecumenical-patriarch-bartholomew-urges-we-must-change-the-way-we-see-the-world-and-society.

Benedict XVI, Pope. *The Word of the Lord* [*Verbum Domini*]. Boston: Pauline, 2010.

Berkman, John, and Michael Cartwright, eds. *The Hauerwas Reader*. Durham, NC: Duke University Press, 2001.

Billy, Dennis. *Contemplative Ethics: An Introduction*. Mahwah, NJ: Paulist, 2011.

Bird, Alexander. "Thomas Kuhn." In *Stanford Encyclopedia of Philosophy*, edited by Edward N. Zalta. https://plato.stanford.edu/archives/spr2022/entries/thomas-kuhn/.

Borghesi, Massimo. *The Mind of Pope Francis: Jorge Mario Bergoglio's Intellectual Journey*. Translated by Barry Hudock. Collegeville, MN: Liturgical, 2018.

———. "The Polarity Model: The Influences of Gaston Fessard and Romano Guardini on Jorge Mario Bergoglio." In *Discovering Pope Francis: The Roots of Jorge Mario Bergoglio's Thinking*, edited by Brian Y. Lee and Thomas Knoebel, 93–113. Collegeville, MN: MN: Liturgical Press Academic, 2019.

Bowden, Nancy Jayne. "'Ma tres chere fille': The Spirituality of Francois de Sales and Jeanne de Chantal and the Enablement of Women." PhD diss., University of Washington, 1995.

Brooks, David. *The Second Mountain: The Quest for a Moral Life*. New York: Random House, 2019.

Brouillette, Andre. "Discerning the Action of God." In *The Holy Spirit: Setting the World on Fire*, edited by Richard Lennan and Nancy Pineda-Madrid, 106–16. New York: Paulist, 2017.

Buckley, James J., and David S. Yeago, eds. *Knowing the Triune God: The Work of the Spirit in the Practices of the Church*. Grand Rapids: Eerdmans, 2001.

Burridge, Richard. *What Are the Gospels? A Comparison with Graeco-Roman Biography*. 2nd ed. Grand Rapids: Eerdmans, 2004.

Carnley, Peter. "Does Receptive Ecumenism Have a Future?" In *Leaning into the Spirit*, edited by Virginia Miller et al., 235–50. Cham: Palgrave Macmillan, 2019.

Carpenter, Angela. *Responsive Becoming: Moral Formation in Theological, Evolutionary, and Developmental Perspective*. London: T. & T. Clark, 2019.

Cassidy, Laurie. "Contemplative Prayer and the Impasse of White Supremacy." In *Desire, Darkness, and Hope: Theology in a Time of Impasse: Engaging the Thought of Constance FitzGerald, OCD*, edited by Laurie Cassidy and M. Shawn Copeland, 103–29. Collegeville, MN: Liturgical Press Academic, 2021.

Catechism of the Catholic Church. Vatican City: Libreria Editrice Vaticana, 1997.

Catholics and United Methodists Together: Shared Prayers and Resources. https://www.unitedmethodistbishops.org/files/websites/www/pdfs/20210209+-+shared+prayers+and+resources%2c+definitive+text.pdf.

Chan, Yiu Sing Lucas. "Biblical Ethics: 3D." In *The Bible and Catholic Theological Ethics*, edited by Yiu Sing Lucas Chan et al., 17–33. Maryknoll, NY: Orbis, 2017.

———. *Biblical Ethics in the 21st Century: Developments, Emerging Consensus, and Future Directions*. New York: Paulist, 2013.

———. *The Ten Commandments and the Beatitudes: Biblical Studies and Ethics for Real Life*. Lanham, MD: Rowman and Littlefield, 2012.

Clifford, Catherine E. "Reform and the Development of Doctrine: An Ecumenical Endeavor." *Jurist* 71 (2011) 35–58.

Clifford, Richard J. "Changing Christian Interpretations of the Old Testament." *Theological Studies* 82 (2021) 509–30.

Clifford, Richard J., and Thomas D. Stegman. "The Christian Bible." In *PBC* 1646–50.

Cloutier, David, and Anthony H. Ahrens. "Catholic Moral Theology and the Virtues: Integrating Psychology in Models of Moral Agency." *Theological Studies* 81 (2020) 326–47.

Cochran, Elizabeth Agnew. "Honesty." In *DSE* 374–75.

Committee on Ecumenical and Interreligious Affairs, United States Conference of Catholic Bishops, and Evangelical Lutheran Church in America. *Declaration on the Way: Church, Ministry and Eucharist*. Minneapolis: Augsburg Fortress, 2015.

Congar, Yves. *I Believe in the Holy Spirit*. Translated by David Smith. New York: Crossroad, 1997.

———. "St. Francis de Sales Today." *Salesian Studies* 3 (1966) 9.

Cook, Jacob Alan. "War, Nonviolence, and Just Peacemaking." In *Discerning Ethics: Diverse Christian Responses to Divisive Moral Issues*, edited by Hak Joon Lee and Tim Dearborn, 183–99. Downers Grove, IL: InterVarsity, 2020.

Cosgrove, Charles H. "Scripture in Ethics: A History." In *DSE* 13–25.

Crisp, Roger, and Michael Slote. "Introduction." In *Virtue Ethics*, edited by Roger Crisp and Michael Slote, 1–25. Oxford: Oxford University Press, 2013.

Crossin, John W. "Building Relationships with Others: The Importance of Reconciliation and Healing." *Catholic Maritime News* 74 (2013) 6–9.

———. "Christian Identities: Necessary but Not Sufficient." *Ecumenical Trends* 38 (2009) 17–30.

———. "Ecumenical Dialogue and Relationships Today: Insights from the Salesian Tradition." In *Human Encounter in the Salesian Tradition*, edited J. F. Chorpenning, 409–23. Rome: International Commission for Salesian Studies, 2007. http://cadeio.org/blog/wp-content/uploads/2014/01/CROSSIN_Talk-on-Friendship.pdf.

———. "Ecumenical Reflections on Moral Discernment." *Journal of Ecumenical Studies* 50 (2015) 561–82.

———. *Friendship: The Key to Spiritual Growth*. New York: Paulist, 1997.

———. "A Meditation on Humility to Honor Archbishop Vsevolod of Scopelos." In *We Are All Brothers*, edited by Jack Figel, 3:181–91. Fairfax, VA: Eastern Christian Publications, 2007.

———. "Moral Actions: The Person Acting and Pope Francis." *Ecumenical Trends* 47 (2018) 71–78.

———. "Moral Anthropology and Human Development." https://washtheocon.org/wp-content/uploads/2013/12/Human-Development.pdf.

———. "Moving Forward in the Spirit: Spirituality and the Search for Christian Unity." *Health Progress*, September–October 2017. https://www.chausa.org/publications/health-progress/article/september-october-2017/moving-forward-in-the-spirit---spirituality-and-the-search-for-christian-unity.

———. "Moving into the Ecumenical Future." *Louvain Studies* 44 (2021) 152–72.

———. "Occasional Reflections on the *Declaration on the Way*." *Ecumenical Trends* 46 (2017) 81–83.

———. "Salesian Spirituality and Adult Developmental Psychology: A Comparative Study of Saint Francis de Sales' Teaching on Virtue and Modern American Developmental Psychology of the Life Cycle." PhD diss., Catholic University of America, 1982.

———. "Virtue as an Ecumenical Ethic." *Ecumenical Trends* 34 (2005) 28–31.

———. *Walking in Virtue: Moral Decisions and Spiritual Growth in Daily Life*. New York: Paulist, 1998.

———. *What Are They Saying about Virtue?* New York: Paulist, 1985.

———. "What Does God Want Us to Do? A Meditation on Discernment." *Ecumenical Trends* 36 (2007) 146–49.

———. "Will Christian Unity Come Sooner Than We Think?" *Ecumenical Trends* 51 (2022) 18–23.

Cunningham, Philip. *Seeking Shalom: The Journey to Right Relationship between Catholics and Jews*. Grand Rapids: Eerdmans, 2015.

Curtis, Brian. "Rebalancing the Bicameral Brain: A Return to Art for Life's Sake." Paper delivered at the SECAC Conference, Greensboro, NC, October 31, 2013.

Dadosky, John. "The Church and the Other: Mediation and Friendship in Post-Vatican II Roman Catholic Ecclesiology." *Pacifica* 18 (2005) 302–22.

———. "The Official Church and the Church of Love in Balthasar's Reading of John: An Exploration in Post-Vatican II Ecclesiology." *Studia Canonica* 41(2007) 453–71.

———. "Towards a Fundamental Theological Interpretation of Vatican II." *Heythrop Journal* 49 (2008) 742–63.

Dailey, Thomas F. "A Song of Prayer: Reading the Canticle of Canticles with St. Francis de Sales." *Studia Mystica* 15 (1992) 65–82.

Davis, Andrew R. "A Biblical View of Covenants Old and New." *Theological Studies* 81 (2020) 631–48.

Dawes, Gregory. "The Interpretation of the Bible." In *NCBC* 16–37.

Dearborn, Tim. "Afterword." In *Discerning Ethics: Diverse Christian Responses to Divisive Moral Issues*, edited by Hak Joon Lee and Tim Dearborn, 317–21. Downers Grove, IL: InterVarsity, 2020.

Delaney, Joan. "From Cremona to Edinburgh: Bishop Bonomelli and the World Missionary Conference of 1910." *The Ecumenical Review* 52 (2009) 418–31.

Delio, Ilia. *Birth of a Dancing Star: From Cradle Catholic to Christian Cyborg*. Maryknoll, NY: Orbis, 2019.

Dicastery for Promoting Christian Unity. "Executive Meeting of the Joint Working Group." http://www.christianunity.va/content/unitacristiani/en/news/2021/2021-10-14-jwg-executive.html.

Domning, Daryl. "Chance, Darwinian Natural Selection, and Why Theology Can't Do without Them." https://washtheocon.org/wp-content/uploads/2013/12/Domning_Darwinian-Natural-Selection.pdf.

Donlon, Thomas. "Oasis of Gentleness in a Desert of Militancy: Francois de Sales's Contribution to French Catholicism." In *Surrender to Christ for Mission: French Spiritual Traditions*, edited by Philip Sheldrake, 90–108. Collegeville, MN: Liturgical, 2018.

———. "Order of the Visitation of Holy Mary: Witness to a Catholicism of *Douceur*." In *Love Is the Perfection of the Mind*, edited by Joseph Chorpenning et al., 35–48. Center Valley, PA: Salesian Center for Faith and Culture, 2017.

———. *The Reform of Zeal: Francois de Sales and Militant French Catholicism*. https://research-repository.st-andrews.ac.uk/bitstream/handle/10023/17415/Donlan_Reform-of-Zeal-St-Andrews-2018.pdf?sequence=1&isAllowed=y.

Dougherty, Rose Mary. *Discernment: A Path to Spiritual Awakening*. New York: Paulist, 2009.

Downs, David. "Vices and Virtues, Lists of." In *DSE* 808–9.

Duffy, Eamon. *John Henry Newman: A Very Brief History*. London: SPCK, 2019.

Duffy, Kathleen. *Teilhard's Mysticism: Seeing the Inner Face of Evolution*. Maryknoll, NY: Orbis, 2014.

———. *Teilhard's Struggle: Embracing the Work of Evolution*. Maryknoll, NY: Orbis, 2019.

Durber, Susan. "Christ's Love Moves the Church: An Ecumenism of the Heart." *The Ecumenical Review* 73 (2021) 364–74.

Ellsberg, Robert. *A Living Gospel: Reading God's Story in Holy Lives*. Maryknoll, NY: Orbis, 2019.

El-Mahassni, Edwin. "Kuhn's Structural Revolution and the Development of Christian Doctrine: A Systematic Discussion." *Heythrop Journal* 59 (2018) 509–22.

Faggioli, Massimo. "Ecclesiology of the Laity in the Global Church." In *The Liminal Papacy of Pope Francis*, 121–28. Maryknoll, NY: Orbis, 2020.

Faith and Order Commission. *Christian Perspectives on Theological Anthropology*. Faith and Order Paper 199. Geneva: WCC, 2014.

———. *Moral Discernment in the Churches: A Study Document*. Faith and Order Paper 215. Geneva: WCC, 2013.

———. *Churches and Moral Discernment*. Vol. 1, *Learning from Traditions*. Edited by Myriam Wijlens and Vladimir Shmaliy. Faith and Order Paper 228. Geneva: WCC, 2021.

————. *Churches and Moral Discernment*. Vol. 2, *Learning from History*. Edited by Myriam Wijlens et al. Faith and Order Paper No. 229. Geneva: WCC, 2021.

————. *Churches and Moral Discernment*. Vol. 3, *Facilitating Dialogue to Build Koinonia*. Faith and Order Paper 235. Geneva: WCC, 2021.

Farrelly, John. M. "Contraception as a Test Case for the Development of Doctrine." *Heythrop Journal* 49 (2008) 453–72.

————. "Holy Spirit." In *New Dictionary of Catholic Spirituality*, edited by Michael Downey, 501–2. Collegeville, MN: Liturgical, 1993.

————. *The Trinity: Recovering the Central Christian Mystery*, 1–29. Lanham, MD: Rowman and Littlefield, 2005.

Fay, Peter K. Review of *The Structure of Theological Revolutions*, by Mark S. Massa. *Socio-Historical Examination of Religion and Ministry* 1 (2019) 327–33.

Fiorelli, Lewis S. "Salesian Understanding of Christian Anthropology." *Salesianum* 46 (1984) 487–508.

Flannery, Austin, ed. *Vatican Council II: The Conciliar and Post Conciliar Documents*. Wilmington, DE: Scholarly Resources, 1975.

Francis, Pope. "Address of His Holiness Pope Francis, June 21, 2019." https://www.vatican.va/content/francesco/en/speeches/2019/june/documents/papa-francesco_20190621_teologia-napoli.html.

————. "Address of His Holiness Pope Francis, January 30, 2021." https://www.vatican.va/content/francesco/en/speeches/2021/january/documents/papa-francesco_20210130_ufficio-catechistico-cei.html.

————. *Evangelii gaudium*. Huntington, IN: Our Sunday Visitor, 2015.

————. *Fratelli tutti*. Washington, DC: United States Conference of Catholic Bishops, 2020.

————. *Gaudete et exsultate*. Boston: Pauline, 2018.

————. *Let Us Dream: A Path to a Better Future*. New York: Simon & Schuster, 2020.

————. *Misericordiae vultus*. http://www.vatican.va/content/francesco/en/apost_letters/documents/papa-francesco_bolla_20150411_misericordiae-vultus.html.

Francis de Sales. *Introduction to the Devout Life*. Translated by John K. Ryan. Garden City, NY: Doubleday, 2003.

————. *Treatise on the Love of God*. Translated by John K. Ryan. 2 vols. Garden City, NY: Doubleday, 1963.

Francis de Sales, and Jane de Chantal. *Letters of Spiritual Direction*. Translated by Peronne Marie Thibert. New York: Paulist, 1988.

Fumagalli, Aristide. "Biblical Ethics and the Proclamation of the Gospel." In *The Bible and Catholic Theological Ethics*, edited by Yiu Sing Lucas Chan et al., 93–105. Maryknoll, NY: Orbis, 2017.

Gaines-Cirelli, Ginger. *Sacred Resistance: A Practical Guide to Christian Witness and Dissent*. Nashville: Abingdon, 2018.

Gibbs, John C. *Moral Development and Reality: Beyond the Theories of Kohlberg, Hoffman, and Haidt*. 4th ed. New York: Oxford University Press, 2019.

Gonzalez, Justo A. *A History of Early Christian Literature*. Louisville: Westminster John Knox, 2019.

Graham, Mark. Review of *Natural Law & Human Dignity*, by Eberhard Schockenhoff. *Theological Studies* 65 (2004) 880–81.

Granberg-Michaelson, Wesley. "Rejecting the Heresy of Individualism." *Sojourners* 1 (2018) 33–35.

Bibliography

Greenberg, Irving. "From Enemy to Partner: Toward the Realization of a Partnership between Judaism and Christianity." In *Nostra Aetate: Celebrating Fifty Years of the Catholic Church's Dialogue with Jews and Muslims*, edited by Pim Valkenberg and Anthony Cirelli, 178–206. Washington, DC: Catholic University of America Press, 2016.

Groppe, Elizabeth. *Yves Congar's Theology of the Holy Spirit*. Oxford: Oxford University Press, 2004.

Hahnenberg, Edward P. *Theology for Ministry: An Introduction for Lay Ministers*. Collegeville, MN: Liturgical, 2014.

Harmon, Steven R. *Baptists, Catholics, and the Whole Church*. Hyde Park, NY: New City, 2021.

———. "Baptist Moral Discernment: Congregational Hearing and Weighing." In F&O, *Churches and Moral Discernment*, edited by Myriam Wijlens and Vladimir Shmaliy, 1:99–114. Geneva: WCC, 2021.

Harrington, Daniel J. *The Gospel of Matthew*. Sacra Pagina Series 1. Collegeville, MN: Liturgical, 2007.

Hauerwas, Stanley. "Virtue." In *WDCE* 648–50.

Haught, John F. *Making Sense of Evolution*. Louisville: Westminster John Knox, 2010.

———. *Resting on the Future: Catholic Theology for an Unfinished Universe*. London: Bloomsbury, 2015.

———. *Science and Faith: A New Introduction*. New York: Paulist, 2012.

Herdt, Jennifer A. *Putting on Virtue: The Legacy of Splendid Vices*. Chicago: University of Chicago Press, 2008.

Hibbs, Thomas S. "Josef Pieper and the Ethics of Virtue." In *A Cosmopolitan Hermit: Modernity and Tradition in the Philosophy of Josef Pieper*, edited by Bernard N. Schumacher, 116–40. Washington, DC: Catholic University of America Press, 2009.

Hocken, Peter. "The Holy Spirit and the Word." *Ecumenical Trends* (2010) 169–75.

Horan, Daniel P. *Catholicity & Emerging Personhood: A Contemporary Theological Anthropology*. Maryknoll, NY: Orbis, 2019.

Hunt, Anne. "Trinity, Christology, and Pneumatology." In *Cambridge Companion to the Trinity*, edited by Peter C. Phan, 365–80. Cambridge: Cambridge University Press, 2011.

International Catholic-Pentecostal Dialogue. "'Do Not Quench the Spirit': Charisms in the Life and Mission of the Church." http://www.christianunity.va/content/unitacristiani/en/dialoghi/sezione-occidentale/pentecostali/dialogo/documenti-di-dialogo/testo-del-documento-in-inglese.html.

International Theological Commission. "Theology Today: Perspectives, Principles, and Criteria." https://www.usccb.org/beliefs-and-teachings/upload/Theology_Today_Perspectives_Principles_Criteria.pdf.

———. "In Search of a Universal Ethic: A New Look at Natural Law." http://www.vatican.va/roman_curia/congregations/cfaith/cti_documents/rc_con_cfaith_doc_20090520_legge-naturale_en.html.

Irvin, Dale T. "The Trinity and Socio-Political Ethics." In *Cambridge Companion to the Trinity*, edited by Peter C. Phan, 398–413. Cambridge: Cambridge University Press, 2011.

Iturrieta, Pablo. Review of *The Structure of Theological Revolutions*, by Mark S. Massa. https://catholicbooksreview.org/2019/massa.html.

Bibliography

John Paul II, Pope. *Novo millennio ineunte*. http://www.vatican.va/content/john-paul-ii/en/apost_letters/2001/documents/hf_jp-ii_apl_20010106_novo-millennio-ineunte.html.

———. *Ut unum sint*. https://www.vatican.va/content/john-paul-ii/en/encyclicals/documents/hf_jp-ii_enc_25051995_ut-unum-sint.html.

Johnson, Luke Timothy. *Decision Making in the Church: A Biblical Model*. Philadelphia: Fortress, 1983.

Joint International Commission for Dialogue between the World Methodist Council and the Roman Catholic Church. *The Call to Holiness: From Glory to Glory*. http://worldmethodistconference.com/wp-content/uploads/2016/01/The-Call-to-Holiness-Final-copy-28062016.pdf.

Kasper, Cardinal Walter. *A Handbook of Spiritual Ecumenism*. Hyde Park, NY: New City, 2007.

Kaveny, Kathleen. *Ethics at the Edges of Law: Christian Moralists and American Legal Thought*. Oxford: Oxford University Press, 2015.

———. *Law's Virtues: Fostering Autonomy and Solidarity in American Society*. Washington, DC: Georgetown University Press, 2012.

Keenan, James. "Foreword." In *Biblical Ethics in the 21st Century*, by Lucas Chan, vii–xiv. New York: Paulist, 2013.

———. *A History of Catholic Moral Theology in the Twentieth Century: From Confessing Sins to Liberating Consciences*. New York: Continuum, 2010.

———. "Introduction." In *The Bible and Catholic Theological Ethics*, edited by Yiu Sing Lucas Chan et al., 1–14. Maryknoll, NY: Orbis, 2017.

Kenneson, Philip. "Gathering: Worship, Imagination, and Formation." In the *Blackwell Companion to Christian Ethics*, edited by Stanley Hauerwas and Samuel Wells, 53–67. Malden, MA: Blackwell, 2006.

Kessler, Diane. "Ecumenical Spirituality: The Quest for Wholeness of Vision." In *The Vision of Christian Unity: Essays in Honor of Paul A. Crow Jr.*, edited by Thomas F. Best and Theodore J. Nottingham, 91–103. Indianapolis: *Oikoumene*, 1997.

Kiesling, Chris A. "Moral Development." In *DSE* 527–28.

Kinnamon, Michael. *Unity as Prophetic Witness: W. A. Visser't Hooft and the Shaping of Ecumenical Theology*. Minneapolis: Fortress, 2018.

Klawans, Jonathan. "The Law." In *The Jewish Annotated New Testament*, edited by Amy-Jill Levine and Marc Zvi Brettler, 515–18. New York: Oxford University Press, 2011.

Koch, Kurt. "Pentecostals, Charismatics and Evangelicals: Impact on the Concept of Unity." http://www.christianunity.va/content/unitacristiani/en/dicastero/assemblee-plenarie/2018-assemblea-plenaria/prolusio-del-cardinale-presidente.html.

———. "What Model of Full Communion?" In *Oxford Handbook of Ecumenical Studies*, edited by Geoffrey Wainwright and Paul McPartlan, 594–609. Oxford: Oxford University Press, 2021.

Kotva, Joseph. *The Christian Case for Virtue Ethics*. Washington, DC: Georgetown University Press, 1996.

Kuhn, Thomas. *The Structure of Scientific Revolutions*. 4th ed. Chicago: University of Chicago Press, 2012.

Ladous, Regis. "Spiritual Ecumenism." In *DEM* 1069–70.

Lee, Brian Y., and Thomas L. Knoebel, eds. *Discovering Pope Francis: The Roots of Jorge Mario Bergoglio's Thinking*. Collegeville, MN: Liturgical Press Academic, 2019.

Bibliography

Lee, Hak Joon. "Introduction." In *Discerning Ethics: Diverse Christian Responses to Divisive Moral Issues*, edited by Hak Joon Lee and Tim Dearborn, 1–14. Downers Grove, IL: InterVarsity, 2020.

Lee, Hak Joon, and Tim Dearborn, eds. *Discerning Ethics: Diverse Christian Responses to Divisive Moral Issues*. Downers Grove, IL: InterVarsity, 2020.

Lennan, Richard, and Nancy Pineda-Madrid, eds. *The Holy Spirit: Setting the World on Fire*. New York: Paulist, 2017.

Logan, Morag. "The Role of Authority in Moral Discernment." In F&O, *Churches and Moral Discernment*, edited by Myriam Wijlens and Vladimir Shmaliy, 1:115–26. Geneva: WCC, 2021.

Lohfink, Gerhard. *Is This All There Is? On Resurrection and Eternal Life*. Translated by Linda M. Maloney. Collegeville, MN: Liturgical, 2018.

Lopresti, Anthony. "Spirituality Meets Ethics: Francis de Sales and Love for God." PhD diss., Boston College, 1999.

Lustig, B. Andrew. "Science and Ethics." In *DSE* 704–8.

Lutheran-Catholic Dialogue Commission for Finland. *Communion in Growth: Declaration on the Church, Eucharist, and Ministry*. https://ecumenism.net/archive/2017_finland_elcf-rcc_communion-in-growth.pdf.

Lux, Otto. "Augustinian Influence in the Ethics of Francis de Sales." *Salesian Studies* 3 (1966) 52–57.

MacIntyre, Alasdair. *After Virtue*. Notre Dame: University of Notre Dame Press, 2007.

Madigan, Patrick. Review of *Natural Law & Human Dignity*, by Eberhard Schockenhoff. *Heythrop Journal* 47 (2006) 492–93.

Massa, Mark S. *The Structure of Theological Revolutions: How the Fight over Birth Control Transformed American Catholicism*. Oxford: Oxford University Press, 2018.

May, William E. *An Introduction to Moral Theology*. 2nd ed. Huntington, IN: Our Sunday Visitor, 2003.

Mayer, Annemarie. "'For a Synodal Church': Equipping the Catholic Church on Her Way into the Third Millennium." *Louvain Studies* 43 (2020) 205–14.

McCarthy, David Matzko. "Truthfulness, Truth-Telling." In *DES* 795–97.

McGoldrick, Terence. "The Living Word: Francis de Sales, a Humanist Biblical Theologian of the Renaissance." In *Love Is the Perfection of the Mind*, edited by Joseph F. Chorpenning et al., 83–101. Center Valley, PA: Salesian Center for Faith and Culture, 2017.

McKenna, Richard John. "The Personal Religious Life in the Thought of St. Francis de Sales." PhD diss., Union Theological Seminary, 1962.

McPartlan, Paul. *Sacrament of Salvation: An Introduction to Eucharistic Ecclesiology*. London: T. & T. Clark, 2005.

McRorie, Christina G. "Moral Reasoning in 'the World.'" *Theological Studies* 82 (2021) 213–37.

McWhorter, Matthew Ryan. Review of *Natural Law & Human Dignity*, by Eberhard Schockenhoff. catholicbooksreview.org/2004/schockenh.htm.

Meier, John P. *A Marginal Jew: Rethinking the Historical Jesus*. 5 vols. Anchor Bible Reference Library. New Haven: Yale University Press, 1991–2016.

Mescher, Marcus. *The Ethics of Encounter: Christian Neighbor Love as a Practice of Solidarity*. Maryknoll, NY: Orbis, 2020.

Messer, Neil. *Theological Neuroethics: Christian Ethics Meets the Science of the Human Brain*. London: T. & T. Clark, 2017.

Miller, Vincent J. "Integral Ecology: Francis's Spiritual and Moral Vision of Interconnectedness." In *The Theological and Ecological Vision of Laudato Si': Everything Is Connected*, edited by Vincent J. Miller, 11–28. London: Bloomsbury T. & T. Clark, 2017.

Miller, Virginia, et al., eds. *Leaning into the Spirit: Ecumenical Perspectives on Discernment and Decision-Making in the Church*. Cham: Palgrave Macmillan, 2019.

Mogenet, Henri. *"Un Aspect de L' 'Humanisme Salesien': Vertus Morales Naturelles et Charite." Revue d'Ascetique to de Mystique* 21 (1940) 114–21.

Moloney, Francis J. *Eucharist as a Celebration of Forgiveness*. Mahwah, NJ: Paulist, 2017.

————. *The Gospel of John*. Sacra Pagina Series 4. Collegeville, MN: Liturgical, 1998.

————. *Love in the Gospel of John: An Exegetical, Theological, and Literary Study*. Grand Rapids: Baker Academic, 2013.

Montague, George T. *Holy Spirit, Make Your Home in Me: Biblical Meditations on Receiving the Gift of the Spirit*. Ijamsville, MD: Word Among Us, 2008.

Morneau, Caitlin, ed. *Harm, Healing, and Human Dignity: A Catholic Encounter with Restorative Justice*. Collegeville, MN: Liturgical, 2019.

Moshman, David. "Foreword." In *Moral Development and Reality: Beyond the Theories of Kohlberg, Hoffman, and Haidt*, by John C. Gibbs, ix–x. New York: Oxford University Press, 2019.

Muers, Rachel, and Kristina Mantasvili. "Introduction." In F&O, *Churches and Moral Discernment*, edited by Myriam Wijlens and Vladimir Shmaliy, 1:xv–xxi. Geneva: WCC, 2021.

Murphey, Nancey, and Warren S. Brown. *Did My Neurons Make Me Do It? Philosophical and Neurobiological Perspectives on Moral Responsibility and Free Will*. Oxford: Oxford University Press, 2008.

Murray, Paul. "The Call of the Spirit to Theological-Ecclesial Renewal: Notes on Being Reasonable and Responsible in Receptive Ecumenical Learning." In *Leaning into the Spirit*, edited by Virginia Miller et al., 217–34. Cham: Palgrave Macmillan, 2019.

O'Collins, Gerald. *The Tripersonal God: Understanding and Interpreting the Trinity*. 2nd ed. New York: Paulist, 2014.

O'Loughlin, Thomas. *The Didache: A Window on the Earliest Christians*. Grand Rapids: Baker Academic, 2010.

O'Malley, John W. *When Bishops Meet: An Essay Comparing Trent, Vatican I, and Vatican II*. Cambridge, MA: Belknap, 2019.

Oberdorfer, Berndt. "Respecting the World, Engaging in the World: Basic Principles of Lutheran Ethics." In F&O, *Churches and Moral Discernment*, edited by Myriam Wijlens and Vladimir Shmaliy, 1:57–69. Geneva: WCC, 2021.

Okey, Stephen. *A Theology of Conversation: An Introduction to David Tracy*. Collegeville, MN: Liturgical, 2018.

Orsy, Ladislas. *Discernment: Theology and Practice, Communal and Personal*. Collegeville, MN: Liturgical, 2020.

Pally, Marcia. *Commonwealth and Covenant: Economics, Politics, and Theologies of Relationality*. Grand Rapids: Eerdmans, 2016.

Parvis, Paul. "Who Was Irenaeus? An Introduction to the Man and His Work." In *Irenaeus: Life, Scripture, Legacy*, edited by Sara Parvis and Paul Foster, 13–24. Minneapolis: Fortress, 2012.

Peters, Rebecca Todd. "Sharing Power to Discern the Will of God in Every Time and Place." In F&O, *Churches and Moral Discernment*, edited by Myriam Wijlens and Vladimir Shmaliy, 1:71–79. Geneva: WCC, 2021.

Phan, Peter C., ed. *The Cambridge Companion to the Trinity*. Cambridge: Cambridge University Press, 2011.

———. "Developments of the Doctrine of the Trinity." In *Cambridge Companion to the Trinity*, edited by Peter C. Phan, 3–12. Cambridge: Cambridge University Press, 2011.

———. "Preface." In *Cambridge Companion to the Trinity*, edited by Peter C. Phan, xiii–xiv. Cambridge: Cambridge University Press, 2011.

———. "Systematic Issues in Trinitarian Theology." In *Cambridge Companion to the Trinity*, edited by Peter C. Phan, 13–29. Cambridge: Cambridge University Press, 2011.

Pieper, Josef. *The Four Cardinal Virtues*. Notre Dame: University of Notre Dame Press, 1966.

Pontifical Biblical Commission. *The Interpretation of the Bible in the Church*. Boston: Pauline Books and Media, 1993.

Pontifical Council for Promoting Christian Unity and Baptist World Alliance. *The Word of God in the Life of the Church*. http://www.christianunity.va/content/unitacristiani/en/dialoghi/sezione-occidentale/alleanza-battista-mondiale/dialogo-internazionale-tra-la-chiesa-cattolica-e-l-alleanza-batt/documenti-di-dialogo/testo-del-documento-in-inglese.html.

Porter, Jean. "The Moral Act in *Veritatis Splendor*." In *The Historical Development of Fundamental Moral Theology in the United States*, edited by Charles E. Curran and Richard A. McCormick, 219–14. New York: Paulist, 1999.

———. *The Perfection of Desire: Habit, Reason, and Virtue in Aquinas' "Summa Theologiae."* Milwaukee: Marquette University Press, 2018.

———. "Virtue Ethics in the Medieval Period." In *The Cambridge Companion to Virtue Ethics*, edited by Daniel C. Russell, 70–91. Cambridge: Cambridge University Press, 2013.

Raiser, Konrad. "Holy Spirit in Ecumenical Thought." In *DEM* 534–41.

Rausch, Thomas. "Ecumenism for a Global Church: Can the Churches of the West and Those of the Global South Learn from Each Other?" In *Leaning into the Spirit*, edited by Virginia Miller et al., 199–216. Cham: Palgrave Macmillan, 2019.

Rinderknecht, Jakob Karl. "Receiving the Joint Declaration: A Test-Case in Bilateral and Multilateral Engagement." *Ecumenical Trends* 49 (2020) 11–15, 26.

Robeck, Cecil M. "Word, Spirit, and Discernment." In F&O, *Churches and Moral Discernment*, edited by Myriam Wijlens and Vladimir Shmaliy, 1:137–45. Geneva: WCC, 2021.

Rohr, Richard. *The Universal Christ: How a Forgotten Reality Can Change Everything We See, Hope For, and Believe*. New York: Convergent, 2019.

Romelt, Joseph. "Catholic Ethical Teaching: Between Infallibility and the Sense of the Faithful." In F&O, *Churches and Moral Discernment*, edited by Myriam Wijlens and Vladimir Shmaliy, 1:37–48. Geneva: WCC, 2021.

Root, Michael. "Morals." In *Oxford Handbook of Ecumenical Studies*, edited by Geoffrey Wainwright and Paul McPartlan, 326–32. Oxford: Oxford University Press, 2021.

Ruedi-Weber, Hans. "Bible, Its Role in the Ecumenical Movement." In *DEM* 108–12.

Rush, Ormond. "A Roman Catholic Commentary on *Walking Together on the Way: Learning to Be the Church—Local, Regional, Universal* of the Anglican–Roman Catholic International Commission." In *Walking Together on the Way: Anglican and Catholic Official Commentaries on the ARCIC Agreed Statement*, 1–30. Great

Britain: SPCK, 2018. http://www.christian unity.va/content/unitacristiani/en/dialoghi/sezione-occidentale/comunione-anglicana/dialogo/arcic-iii/arcic-iii—-documents/2018-walking-together-on-the-way—-commentary.html.

Salzman, Todd A. *What Are They Saying about Catholic Ethical Method?* New York: Paulist, 2003.

Salzman, Todd A., and Michael G. Lawler. *Virtue and Theological Ethics: Toward a Renewed Ethical Method.* Maryknoll, NY: Orbis, 2018.

Sanford, Jonathan J. *Before Virtue: Assessing Contemporary Virtue Ethics.* Washington, DC: Catholic University of America Press, 2019.

Sauca, Ioan. "God Is Love—The Experience of the Just, Compassionate, and Merciful God: Ecumenical Considerations Inspired by Orthodox Spirituality on the Theme of the Karlsruhe Assembly of the World Council of Churches." *Ecumenical Review* 73 (2021) 349–63.

Savary, Louis M. *Teilhard de Chardin on Morality: Living in an Evolving World.* New York: Paulist, 2019.

Schaefer, Jame. "Keeping Scientifically Informed: A Duty for Theologians and the Church Magisterium." *CTSA Proceedings* 75 (2021) 178–84.

Schemenauer, Kevin. "Guide Them All: St. Francis de Sales on Cultivating the Love of God." In *A Science of the Saints: Studies in Spiritual Direction*, edited by Robert E. Alvis, 72–93. Collegeville, MN: Liturgical, 2020.

Schockenhoff, Eberhard. *Natural Law & Human Dignity: Universal Ethics in an Historical World.* Washington, DC: Catholic University of America Press, 2003.

Schumacher, Bernard N. "A Cosmopolitan Hermit: An Introduction to the Philosophy of Josef Pieper." In *A Cosmopolitan Hermit: Modernity and Tradition in the Philosophy of Josef Pieper*, edited by Bernard N. Schumacher, 1–23. Washington, DC: Catholic University of America Press, 2009.

Second Vatican Council. *Dei Verbum.* https://www.vatican.va/archive/hist_councils/ii_vatican_council/documents/vat-ii_const_19651118_dei-verbum_en.html.

Senior, Donald. *Raymond E. Brown and the Catholic Biblical Renewal.* New York: Paulist, 2018.

Senn, Simone. "Introduction." In F&O, *Churches and Moral Discernment*, edited by Myriam Wijlens et al., 2:xiii–xxiv. Geneva: WCC, 2021.

Sider, Ron. *Speak Your Peace: What the Bible Says about Loving Our Enemies.* Harrisonburg, VA: Herald, 2020.

Simpson, Peter L. "Have You Tried Scotus? Aquinas Didn't Know Everything." *Commonweal*, June 14, 2019.

Sommers, Mary C. Review of *Natural Law & Human Dignity*, by Eberhard Schockenhoff. *The Thomist* 69 (2005) 153–57.

Special Commission appointed by Ecumenical Patriarch Bartholomew I. *For the Life of the World: Toward a Social Ethos of the Orthodox Church.* https://www.goarch.org/social-ethos.

Spohn, William. *Go and Do Likewise: Jesus and Ethics.* New York: Continuum, 1999.

———. "Scripture." In *Oxford Handbook of Theological Ethics*, edited by Gilbert Meilaender and William Werpehowski, 93–111. Oxford: Oxford University Press, 2005.

Stassen, Glen H. "Sermon on the Mount." In *DSE* 715–17.

Still, Walter Karl. "Natural Law Theory in Roman Catholic Theology: A Paradigm to Remedy the Crisis in the Contemporary Lutheran Ethic?" PhD diss., Duquesne University, 2003.

Stopp, Elisabeth. "St. Francis de Sales: Attitudes to Friendship." In *A Man to Heal Differences: Essays and Talks on St. Francis de Sales*, 119–38. Philadelphia: Saint Joseph's University Press, 1997.

Strong, Barry R. *The Economy of the Spirit in Ecumenical Perspective*. Rome: Pontificia Universitas Gregoriana, 1991.

Swanton, Christine. "The Definition of Virtue Ethics" In the *Cambridge Companion to Virtue Ethics*, edited by Daniel C. Russell, 315–38. Cambridge: Cambridge University Press, 2013.

Tavard, George H. "Tradition." In *NDT* 1037–41.

Therese, Lisa. "Salesian Discernment." *Indian Journal of Spirituality* 30 (2017) 201–12.

Thomasset, Alain. "The Virtue of Hospitality according to the Bible and the Challenge of Migration." In *The Bible and Catholic Theological Ethics*, editors Yiu Sing Lucas Chan et al., 34–44. Maryknoll, NY: Orbis, 2017.

Tousley, Nikki Coffey, and Brad J. Kallenberg. "Virtue Ethics." In *DSE* 814–19.

Ulanowicz, Robert E. "Mutualism in the Darwinian Scenario." https://washtheocon.org/wp-content/uploads/2013/12/Mutualism-Darwinian.pdf.

Vacek, Edward Collins. "Discernment within a Mutual Love Relationship with God: A New Theological Foundation." *Theological Studies* 74 (2013) 683–710.

Vicini, Andrea. "Empowered by the Holy Spirit." In *The Holy Spirit: Setting the World on Fire*, edited by Richard Lennan and Nancy Pineda-Madrid, 162–72. New York: Paulist, 2017.

Vondey, Wolfgang. *Pentecostal Theology: Living the Full Gospel*. London: Bloomsbury T. & T. Clark, 2017.

———. "The Unity and Diversity of Pentecostal Theology: A Brief Account for the Ecumenical Community in the West." *Ecclesiology* 10 (2014) 76–100.

Wadell, Paul J. *Becoming Friends: Worship, Justice, and the Practice of Christian Friendship*. Grand Rapids: Brazos, 2002.

———. "Friendship, Friendship Ethics." In *DSE* 316–18.

Walter, James J. "Virtue." In *NDT* 1081–85.

Ward, Thomas M. "Voluntarism, Atonement, and Duns Scotus." *Heythrop Journal* 58 (2017) 37–43.

Ware, Kallistos. "Tradition and Traditions." In *DEM* 1143–48.

Washington Theological Consortium. "Religion and Science in Pastoral Ministry." https://washtheocon.org/resources/using-science-pastoral-ministry/.

Wayman, Benjamin D. "Imagining the Future of Theological Education: Conversations with Four Theologians." *Christian Century*, February 10, 2021. https://www.christiancentury.org/article/features/imagining-future-theological-education.

Werntz, Myles. "Prayerful Resistance: Howard Thurman's Contemplative Nonviolence." *Christian Century*, August 15, 2019.

Wicks, Jared. *Investigating Vatican II: Its Theologians, Ecumenical Turn, and Biblical Commitment*. Washington, DC: Catholic University of America Press, 2018.

Wijlens, Myriam, and Vladimir Somali. "Preface." In F&O, *Churches and Moral Discernment*, edited by Myriam Wijlens et al., 2:ix–xii. Geneva: WCC, 2021.

Williams, Rowan. "Introduction." In *Living Dialogue: Steps on the Way to Communion among Christians*, by Chiara Lubich, 11–12. Hyde Park, NY: New City, 2009.

———. *Luminaries: Twenty Lives That Illuminate the Christian Way*. London: SPCK, 2019.

Bibliography

Wilson-Hargrove, Jonathan. *Reconstructing the Gospel: Finding Freedom from Slaveholder Religion*. Downers Grove, IL: InterVarsity, 2018.

Witherup, Ronald D. "The Bible in the Life of the Church." In *PBC* 1615–20.

———. *Scripture: Dei Verbum*. Rediscovering Vatican II. New York: Paulist, 2006.

———. "The Theme of the Letter: Faith and Works (2:15–21)." In *Galatians: Life in the New Creation, A Spiritual-Pastoral Reading*, 51–60. New York: Paulist, 2020.

Wood, Susan, and Timothy J. Wengert. "The Path to the Joint Declaration on the Doctrine of Justification." In *A Shared Spiritual Journey: Lutherans and Catholic Traveling toward Unity*, 34–66. New York: Paulist, 2016.

World Council of Churches, et al. *Christian Witness in a Multi-Religious World: Recommendations for Conduct*. https://www.oikoumene.org/sites/default/files/Document/ChristianWitness_recommendations.pdf.

Worthen, Jeremy. "Anglican Moral Discernment: Sources, Structures, and Dynamics of Authority." In F&O, *Churches and Moral Discernment*, edited by Myriam Wijlens and Vladimir Shmaliy, 1:81–90. Geneva: WCC, 2021.

Wright, Wendy M. *Bond of Perfection: Jeanne de Chantal & Francois de Sales*. Enhanced ed. Stella Niagara, NY: DeSales Resource Center, 2007.

Zacharias, Ronaldo. "From Absolute Trust and Systematic Suspicion to a Hermeneutics of Appreciation." In *The Bible and Catholic Theological Ethics*, edited by Yiu Sing Lucas Chan et al., 273–85. Maryknoll, NY: Orbis, 2017.

Subject Index

Name Index

Name Index

Vondey, Wolfgang, 3n4

Wadell, Paul J., 38n9
Wainwright, Geoffrey, 118
Walter, James J., 76n8
Ward, Thomas M., 11n35
Ware, Kallistos, 28n12
Wengert, Timothy J., 52, 52nn12–13, 54, 54n17, 57, 57n25, 143n1
Werntz, Myles, 99, 99n36, 100n37
Wesley, John, 75, 109, 111
Wicks, Jared, 25, 25n3
Wijlens, Myriam, 116, 116n41
Willebrands, Johannes, 57
Williams, Rowan, 36, 36nn4–5, 50, 77n9

Wilson-Hargrove, Jonathan, 102, 102n46, 103
Witherup, Ronald J., 28, 28n12, 71n25
Wittgenstein, Ludwig, 89
Wood, Susan K., 52, 52nn12–13, 54, 54n17, 57, 57n25, 143n1
Worthen, Jeremy, 109, 109n13, 109n15, 110, 110n19, 111, 111n23, 112, 112n27, 112n30
Wright, Wendy M., 38n11

Yeago, David S., 8nn19–20

Zacharias, Renaldo, 33
Zizioulas, John, 9